D0985690

DIALOGUE AT WORK

The Mike Pedler Library
Developing people and organizations
General Editor: Dr Mike Pedler

Books published simultaneously in this series:

Reg Revans
ABC of Action Learning

Nancy M. Dixon
Dialogue at Work

Mike Pedler and Kath Aspinwall
A Concise Guide to the Learning Organization

Rennie Fritchie and Malcolm Leary
Resolving Conflicts in Organizations

Would you like to receive regular information about forthcoming new books in the Mike Pedler Library? Would you like to send us your comments about the book you have read? If so, we would be very pleased to hear from you.

Lemos & Crane
20 Pond Square
Highgate Village
London N6 6BA
England
Tel   +44(0)181 348 8263
Fax   +44(0)181 347 5740
Email admin@lemos.demon.co.uk

Dialogue At Work

NANCY M. DIXON

Lemos&Crane

This edition first published in Great Britain 1998
Lemos & Crane
20 Pond Square
Highgate
London N6 6BA

© Center for Creative Leadership 1996 and Nancy Dixon 1998

The right of Nancy Dixon to be identified as the author of this work has been asserted in accordance with the Copyright, Designs and Patents Act 1988. Except for the quotation of short passages for the purposes of criticism and review, no part of this publication may be reproduced, stored in a retrieval system, or transmitted, in any form or by any means, electronic, mechanical, photocopying, recording or otherwise, without prior permission from the publishers. All rights reserved. Chapters 1 to 6 of this edition first published in 1996 by the Center for Creative Leadership, PO Box 26300, Greensboro, North Carolina, USA as *Perspectives on Dialogue*.

ISBN 1-898001-41-3

A CIP catalogue record for this book is available from the British Library.

Designed and typeset by DAP Ltd, London
Printed and Bound by Redwood Books, Trowbridge.

Contents

Introduction to the Library .... *vii*

Foreword .... *xiii*

Acknowledgements .... *xiv*

1. INTRODUCTION *1*

2. TALK AND DEVELOPMENT *5*

3. FIVE PERSPECTIVES ON DIALOGUE FOR DEVELOPMENT *19*

4. PRACTICAL OBSERVATIONS ON DIALOGUE *57*

5. HOW DIALOGUE CAN BE INCORPORATED
                                        INTO WORK PRACTICES *71*

6. FORUMS AND CONDITIONS FOR DIALOGUE *83*

7. DIALOGUE PRACTICES IN ORGANIZATIONS *97*

    Index *131*

Introduction to the Library

"All learning is for the sake of action, and all action for the sake of friendship." John Macmurray

At the end of centuries and especially millennia, all manner of prophecies break out and gain hold in the public imagination. The world of business and management is no exception to this law as it entertains a great variety of excited ideas for dealing with the better ordering of business and corporate affairs in the face of the supposed end of certainty and, with this, the arts of prediction and strategic planning. In their place we are offered notions of paradox, of chaos and boundlessness, of multiple dilemmas and complexity theory. And these are merely at the "softer" end; at the other there is much old wine in new bottles as the nostrums of Taylorism and Fordism suffuse the apparently novel re-engineering and quality movements.

The value of learning

To be responsive to change, a child, adult, organization, even a society, must be adept at learning. Learning is the means not only of acquiring new knowledge and skill but also of making sense of our lives - individually and collectively - in increasingly fragmented times. We may not know "the how" of this or that, but we can go on hopefully in pursuit of learning a way through. In the absence of a plan, a blueprint for success, we can learn our way forward, growing in confidence as to what we can do and in who we are, making our own path.

For organizations, with an average lifespan of 40 years and declining, learning has become essential for survival

(De Geus). Organizational learning has also been suggested as the only sustainable source of competitive advantage (Senge) and the single most important quality which can be developed and traded (Garratt).

At community or society level new efforts at collaborative action and learning in public forums to tackle the "wicked" problems of poverty, inequality, pollution, crime and public safety look so much more relevant than the old questions of left or right, public or private, electoral democracy or entrepreneurial leadership.

For societies, communities, organizations and individuals the questions are similar: how can we develop those things which we do best so as to be able to trade, exchange, learn, whilst not shutting our eyes to the downsides, shadows, problems and consequences? How can we release energy, potential, self-reliability and active citizenship and build wealth, well-being, collective security, welfare, public services and generally improve the quality of our lives?

A Learning Society?

In an era characterised by large organizations and complexity, it has become plain that individual learning, however impressive, cannot alone resolve problems in relationships - be they at personal, team or organizational level. Equally, it is becoming clear that even the very best of our organizations, private or public, cannot alone resolve the intractable issues of communities and societies. The idea of the "learning organization" is a recognition of, and one response to, the limits of individual learning. But more is needed; there are urgent tasks to hand which go beyond the scope and remit of any single organization or coalition of agencies. As touched on above, these issues demand the organization of action and learning in a different context, and one which is scarcely yet glimpsed, yet alone grasped. In such an ideal collaboration as a Learning Society, there is:

- The freedom to learn - or not to learn - for individuals.

- An organizational aim to support the learning of all members and stakeholders and a desire to transform the organization, as a whole and when appropriate, in creating new products, services and relationships.

- A social drive to provide equality of opportunity for learning to all citizens, at least partly in order that they might contribute to that society being a good place to live in.

The links in this collaborative ideal can be represented diagramatically as follows:

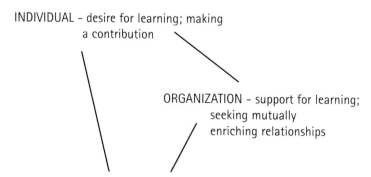

INDIVIDUAL - desire for learning; making a contribution

ORGANIZATION - support for learning; seeking mutually enriching relationships

COMMUNITY/SOCIETY - equal opportunities for learning; providing a good place to live

This manifesto is of course a re-interpretation of old revolutionary aspirations - Liberty (for individuals), the ruling value of Fraternity for organizations, and a duty of Equality of treatment and opportunity in the social sphere.

To each of these we hope to make a contribution, without being confined or encompassed by ideas of personal self-development, or of organizational change, learning, and transformation, nor yet by those of community development or social policy. If a book focuses on, say, organizational processes, then it also keeps an eye on the personal and social development aspects; if it is primarily aimed at the self-development of individuals, then this is in the context of working in organizations and living in society.

The books in the Library are concerned with learning and action on such pressing issues facing us as people working in organizations, living in communities, cities and societies. And whilst there is no single philosophy here, there is an implied criticism of the economic and cultural consensus which underlies much business and management literature in particular. There are challenges here for those who tend to assume that our future rests on the "roll out" of global, information-based capitalism supported by the spread of liberalism and democracy. There is support here for those who question whether individual or organizational development aimed at "high performance" or "excellence" inevitably leads only to desirable outcomes. Here, the irony of the self-proclaimed "learning organization" that is still not a healthy place for people to work in or to live next to, is noted. Here is an aspiration to engage our "best and brightest" and our talent for organizing with some of the really difficult and intractable issues facing us. Above all, we seek to be inclusive and to sustain and support all those trying to learn new things in order to act differently in pursuit of friendship.

Beyond ideas to useful action

Because action and learning require more than just good ideas, the Library is characterised by two more "laws of three". In terms of content, each book contains:

- *educational input* - ideas of substance that you need to know about.

- *invitations to action* - at various points it is suggested that you need to stop and to actually do something with the ideas in order to learn.

- *ethical or political elements* - being an honest colleague, doing the "right thing", seeking good purposes or responding to difficult tasks and circumstances usually imply ethical dilemmas or struggle and perhaps the need for moral support in action and learning.

In terms of pitch or level, though they aim to be attractive and accessible, these books are not "easy reads". Not content with theories and suspicious of easy answers, tools and techniques, these books offer a middle ground of active methods and approaches to the problems and questions posed. Here is an invitation to self-confrontation for the reader. Aware of the complexity and of the questions to which there are no answers, nevertheless there are ways forward, structures to use, directions to follow in order to engage your own energies, the ingenuity of colleagues and the aspirations of customers or those you serve in order to learn your way through. You can't put such a book down without at least thinking of doing something differently.

MIKE PEDLER

FOREWORD

Nancy Dixon is that rare combination of scholar and practitioner. Her ideas are strongly based on research whilst being accessible and of practical use. A teacher and researcher at George Washington University, she is also a highly regarded consultant to government and business organizations. Nancy has studied with Chris Argyris in the USA and Reg Revans in the UK and her practice has evolved from her learning and knowledge of action learning and action science.

Her 1994 book *The Organizational Learning Cycle* was described by David Kolb as the best book on organizational learning he had read. Her contribution to this series, *Dialogue At Work,* continues in the same vein of high quality. Here Nancy draws upon a deep understanding of the literature and distils this into practical advice on how to go about improving dialogue for the development of people and organizations. This is radical yet sound and essential advice for anyone who is serious about moving towards the learning organization.

MIKE PEDLER

ACKNOWLEDGEMENTS

This book has benefited from the helpful review of many people. I would like to especially thank the following: Robert Burnside, Bill Drath, Cynthia Graham, Jack Mezirow, Charles Palus, James Rush, and Ellen Van Velsor.

1 Introduction

There is a growing sense today that organizations and the people that make them up are, to repeat a figure of speech used by Robert Kegan, "in over their heads". As diversity becomes the rule and change the sole constant, complexity is increasing. The only effective response to this complexity is development: both at the individual level and at the organizational level.

Consequently, a great deal of effort is now being devoted to individual and organizational development. One developmental activity, which is much practised but imperfectly understood, takes place at the intersection between these levels: talk.

Not all talk is developmental, of course. In this book I will first discuss the relationship between talk and development in organizations, looking at the basic ways that developmental talk - or, as it is often referred to, dialogue - differs from the skilled talk that goes on all the time. I will next summarize five perspectives on dialogue as offered by leading theorists, and in Chapter 4 make a series of practical observations based on these views. I will review in Chapter 5 some examples of how dialogue has been incorporated into the work processes of organizations. In Chapter 6, I discuss the conditions for dialogue and the forums for dialogue, including future search conferences, open space technology, action learning, real-time strategic change and team syntegrity.

In the final chapter, I examine the ways dialogue is being used in organizations, as well as methods to introduce and improve dialogue.

This book is meant primarily for human resources professionals and practising managers who are responsible for individual and organizational development, but it should also be of interest to anyone who is concerned with development.

Perhaps like many authors, I have written this as much for myself as I have to communicate my ideas to others. For me, writing has often been a way to clarify my own thinking or to make sense of a difficult issue with which I am wrestling. Dialogue fits well into my category of difficult issues.

I have been struck by the enthusiasm people express for dialogue. Over the last few years dialogue groups have formed around the United States and dialogue seminars have sprung up. The term "dialogue" is now frequently heard when the speaker wants to convey that the discussion will be in greater depth or will be more real than usual. Yet, as I listen to conversations between organizational members or sit in meetings in organizations, I hear very little that I would call dialogue going on. It is the near absence of something we seem to find so appealing that perplexes me. Is it that we lack the skills to have a dialogue? Do we need more training courses in listening or communication? Or do we already know how to dialogue but are constrained by the organizations in which we function so that we are unable to do what we know how to do? I have resided on both sides of that quandary.

On the "we lack the necessary skills" side, I have given courses that teach Argyris' Model II skills for many years at the university. Although the skills are difficult to learn and can, at times, be very frustrating, these courses are, without doubt, the ones my students say they find most valuable. They learn a set of skills that they say impact not only their work life, but their personal life as well. I have been intrigued by the way change happens in those learners. They make a significant change not when they have mastered the technique, which can take up to a year, but when they have internalized the values represented in the technique. The skills themselves are like a door that allows them to reach the values.

On the side of "it's the situation that constrains us", for many years I led Great Books discussion groups. We didn't teach skills in how to dialogue in Great Books, but there were some strict rules we followed in those discussions such as: no one could talk unless he or she had read the book we were discussing; no one could refer to an outside authority, we all spoke only from our own understanding of what we had read; the leader, who framed the questions under discussion, was limited to asking questions for which she truly had no answer herself. Those rules, and others, created the conditions which allowed a rich and meaningful dialogue to take place.

Having experienced both sides of the conundrum without finding a satisfying resolution, I have returned to many of the theorists who have influenced my thinking about dialogue to look for answers. As you will read, what I have come away with is a reframing of the issue that is based more in the way we relate to each other than with either our skill level or the conditions under which we employ them.

2. Talk and Development

IN THIS CHAPTER: *Talk is the most frequent activity among managers but how can it lead to learning and development?*

Contents

INDIVIDUAL DEVELOPMENT   *p. 8*

ORGANIZATIONAL DEVELOPMENT   *p. 10*

DEVELOPMENT AS A NECESSARY
            RESPONSE TO COMPLEXITY   *p. 11*

DIALOGUE: DEVELOPMENT TALK   *p. 13*

 Sources   *p. 17*

2 Talk and Development

As a number of studies have documented,[1] talk is the most frequent activity of managers. Some say that as much as 75 per cent of a manager's day is spent in conversation.[2]

Yet, for all this, there is a sense that something is wrong with the way people talk to each other at work - something is artificial, false, or at least unsatisfying much of the time. They often think to themselves that they have to be careful about what they say and to whom they say it. There are things that might be said privately, to a trusted colleague, which cannot be said publicly. On the other hand, people sometimes say something publicly that they realize they do not really believe; it is said "just for show". Organizational talk often has a game-like quality that makes it seem unreal.

I believe that people long for a more authentic kind of interaction with their co-workers but that they are not sure that it is possible, or even if their longing is legitimate. Work is not generally thought of as a place where you are supposed to get your own needs met. Thus, people come to accept what they believe to be inevitable, that they must leave a part of themselves at home when they come to work.

What is lost, when talk is limited in these ways, are two kinds of development. Individuals lose the opportunity to learn in ways that could foster their growth. If they cannot be themselves at work, they cannot develop themselves at work and the organization, the system as a whole, loses the opportunity to learn those things about itself and about its interaction with its environment that could lead to its development.

INDIVIDUAL DEVELOPMENT

Open, differentiated and integrated perspectives

There is substantial agreement among development theorists that individual development is, potentially, life long rather than ending with adulthood. Although these theorists differ greatly about what comprises various stages, or even if stages are an appropriate frame, they generally agree about the direction that adult development takes.[3] Given both challenge and support, individual adults take on an increasingly more open, differentiated, and integrated perspective. "Open", in this context, means a willingness to entertain alternative perspectives. "Differentiated" means the individual is able to draw finer distinctions between concepts (for example, the concept of "team" can be differentiated into self-directed and manager-led or, alternatively, into task teams, performing teams, production teams, and so on, each having distinguishing characteristics that result in different issues). "Integrated" means that the individual is able to weave these differences into an increasingly complex whole, a system view rather than an ethnocentric or fragmented view. As an individual becomes more developed he or she is able to deal with increasing complexity - or, perhaps more accurately, is able to construct increasingly more complex perspectives on the world. The opposite of continued adult development is rigid and highly defended thought patterns - patterns that leave a person less able to adapt to changing conditions and less able to change.

Support for re-framing

Adult development is, however, only a potential; it is not a certainty. For development to occur an individual must continue to face new issues or problems for which current responses are inadequate. In order to deal with new challenges the person must re-frame his or her understanding of "self in the world" or "self in relation to the system" of which the individual is a part. It is, of course, quite distressing to find that one's current understanding of "self in the world" is inadequate, that one doesn't yet "have it figured out." So an individual in the midst of development must have the support of others, both to sustain the effort and to offer alternative frames.

Organizations, however, are in general poor places to develop. People can develop specialization in them. There are adequate challenges and support for re-framing within an area of technical skill or abstract concepts. But when it comes to developing themselves more broadly, the way people talk to each other (avoiding open exchange, trying to win at all costs, and other tendencies described below) can prevent them from receiving the information and support that is necessary for re-framing.

ORGANIZATIONAL DEVELOPMENT

Defensive routines

Organizations also acquire patterns of interaction that can make it difficult for the system as a whole to find out about itself and thus to develop. Chris Argyris has referred to these patterns as "defensive routines".[4] These are customary ways of acting that the organization evolves to avoid embarrassment or conflict. For example, people frequently modify information that is sent upward through the organization so that it appears more favourable, and subordinates often agree to do a task or carry out a process that they believe will not work. Defensive routines work in the sense that they do prevent embarrassment and conflict, but in so doing they also prevent the organization from learning about challenges which, if faced directly, could lead to new ways of thinking - that is, could lead to development.

Learning and development

I believe that both individual and organizational development are dependent upon learning and that learning is dependent upon talk; thus, talk leads to learning, which leads to development. Obviously, though, not all talk leads to learning. As I have just pointed out, some talk may indeed work against it. (It is also important to note that learning can and does occur without talk - for example, learning calculus from a computer programme, learning history from a text. However, the learning in which I am interested here is the kind I referred to above: learning that results in an individual or system re-framing self in relation to the world.)

DEVELOPMENT AS A NECESSARY RESPONSE TO COMPLEXITY

Robert Kegan has defined development as:

> *"the active process of increasingly organizing the relationship of the self to the environment. The relationship gets better organized by increasing differentiations of the self from the environment and thus by increasing integrations of the environment."*[5]

At a systems level, Ashby's law of requisite variety,[6] which states that the internal regulatory mechanisms of a system must be as diverse as the environment with which it is trying to deal, is again an argument for differentiation and integration - or the development of the organization as an ever-more-complex system.

Organizational responses

To live in a world that is culturally diverse requires individuals to be more complex than to live in a homogeneous world. People face diversity every day as organizations become more heterogeneous and struggle with ensuing issues of equity and fairness. The women and people of colour who are exiting corporations in increasing numbers speak to the current ineptitude in addressing the complexity that cultural diversity brings with it.[7] As organizations become more global, people must deal with yet wider issues of cultural diversity: fairness in wages and benefits within poorer countries, disruption of family patterns in traditional countries, and economic exploitation juxtaposed against national loyalty, to name only a few.

11

To live in a fast-changing environment requires greater complexity than to live in a more stable world. The speed with which product decisions must be made often prevents considered thought of their consequences. The technological advances that make possessions quickly obsolete create environmental problems and issues of equity about the use of the planet's scarce resources. The organizational changes that force people frequently to change tasks, colleagues, and location leave them bereft of community and support. Einstein's insight that the world that people have made as a result of the level of thinking they have done thus far creates problems that cannot be solved at the same level as they were created, makes the case for development.

This is an age in which people are aware that their truths are embedded within a paradigm that, over time, will surely be transcended. This consciousness requires more complexity than living in a world in which truth is sure and steadfast. Some have said that this may be the first generation that is fully aware that it functions within a paradigm - that knowledge is ephemeral and conditional. Theorists such as Thomas Kuhn[8] and Peter Berger[9] have carefully illustrated how people construct their own reality. That is a difficult fate - not to have truth - to labour in the great vineyard of constructed reality. It requires much greater complexity than many have been able to develop. Robert Kegan[10] was right: people find themselves in over their heads much of the time.

The organizations where people work are also in over their heads. They are actively searching for new ways of acting and interacting. There is a growing acknowledgement that organizations cannot face this increased level of complexity armed with the traditional tools of bureaucracy: control, consistency, and predictability.[11] Organizations are actively seeking new ways of interacting, such as empowerment, self-directed teams, and organizational learning. They are, as well, seeking new forms of structure - for instance, Handy's shamrock organization[12] and Ackoff's democratic corporation[13].

Individual and organizational development is a long-term answer to dealing with increased complexity, not a quick fix. Development moves at its own pace. It can be stifled, as it regularly is in current organizations, but it is difficult to hurry. The best that can be done is to make organizations places where individuals can know themselves and speak their truth.

DEVELOPMENTAL TALK

I suggested above that if people cannot be themselves at work, they cannot develop themselves at work. They may fail to be themselves by:

- misleading others in what they say;
- saying more than they know; or
- saying nothing.

Being oneself at work means that the person speaks authentically, agreeing and disagreeing, voicing one's hopes and distresses. Individual development is about taking on an increasingly open, differentiated, and integrated perspective. To do that the person must give voice to his or her current perspective so that others can respond to it. Then in talking with others, reflecting an authentic self, the person learns from others about his or her tacit assumptions and, if those assumptions prove to be no longer viable, may choose to change them - to develop. Thus, speaking out of one's own experience, he or she may hear that experience affirmed by others, perhaps in more eloquent words, and come to understand it more fully - to develop. Similarly, the person can internalize the perspectives of others, and integrate their ideas with his or her own - develop. Carl Jung said,[14]

> *"I can only make direct statements, only 'tell stories.'*
> *Whether or not the stories are 'true' is not the*
> *problem. The only question is whether what I tell is*
> *my fable, my truth."*

Developmental talk requires each person to say his or her own truth - not *the* truth but his or her own truth. And in giving voice to that truth, each person opens the door to his or her development. I do not want to be misunderstood as advocating that people should say everything that comes into their heads, that they should be "brutally honest". I am not suggesting that it is necessary to give voice to every thought in order to be authentic or to develop. It is, however, necessary to speak authentically and fully about all which bears upon the subject of the dialogue. To do less is to mislead others who are trying to learn, and to prevent oneself from learning as well.

Saying more than one knows

Another way people can limit their development is by saying more than they know. It is difficult to avoid this, particularly when a person is placed in an authority role by virtue of position or expertise. Morris Cohen, in speaking facetiously about professors, once said, "No man, however conservative, can stand before a class day after day and refrain from saying more than he knows." I could paraphrase that to say, "No manager, however conservative, can talk with subordinates day after day and refrain from saying more than he or she knows." When individuals say more than they know they lose the ability to hear the perspectives of others, and others, hearing that person's certainty, refrain from offering their conflicting thoughts, which might widen and enrich his or her perspective. Paulo Freire reminded us of the need for humility in talking with each other when he said,

> "The encounter of men addressed to the common task
> of learning and acting . . . is broken if the parties (or
> one of them) lack humility. How can I [talk
> developmentally with others] if I always project
> ignorance onto others and never perceive my own?"

In developmental talk a person is not obliged to say more than he or she knows. The task is not to convince, sell, or get "buy in". A person can, even as a manager or expert, speak his or her own truth, without claiming it as the truth.

Saying nothing

Silence, which in practical terms is the opposite of saying more than one knows, is equally debilitating to development. Audre Lorde, the black feminist poet, has written eloquently about silence.

> "I have come to believe over and over again that what
> is most important to me must be spoken, made verbal
> and shared, even at the risk of having it bruised or
> misunderstood. That the speaking profits me, beyond
> any other effect." [15]

People break their silence because it profits them, in their own growth and development and in the development of others.

★

People become what they act out, conditioning themselves by their play-acting. If, day by day, they act indifferent when they really hurt for others, disinterested when they are truly ashamed, stoical when inside they are joyous, then, over time, they will become indifferent, disinterested, and stoical. If, on the other hand, the situation is such that they can act authentically, openly, and in relationship with others, then they have the opportunity to develop into authentic, open people who deal with others in relationship and not as objects.

The kind of talk that I have just described has been called "dialogue". There are a number of theorists who have thought very carefully about the nature of dialogue. Let's review their ideas and see what can be learned from them about how people might talk in ways that are more meaningful at work.

SOURCES FOR CHAPTER 2

[1] Kotter J P (1990) *A Force for Change* Free Press, New York; Mintzberg H (1973) *The Nature of Managerial* Work Prentice Hall, Englewood Cliffs NJ; Stewart R (1985) *The Reality of Management* (2nd edn) Heinemann, London.

[2] For instance, Gronn P C (1983) 'Talk As the Work: the accomplishment of school administration' *Administrative Science Quarterly* 28(1), 1-2.

[3] Commons M L, Richards F A and Armon C (eds) (1984) *Beyond Formal Operations: late adolescent and adult cognitive development* Praeger, New York; Kegan R (1994) *In Over Our Heads* Harvard University Press, Cambridge Ma; Labouvie-Vief G (1984) 'Logic and Self-Regulation from Youth to Maturity: a model' in Commons M L et al (1984) *ibid*; Perry W G (1970) *Forms of Intellectual and Ethical Development in College Years: a scheme* Holt Reinehart & Winston, New York.

[4] Argyris C (1990) *Overcoming Organizational Defenses: facilitating organizational learning* Allyn & Bacon, Boston.

[5] Kegan R (1994) *ibid*, p.114.

[6] Ashby W R (1960) *An Introduction to Cybernetics* Wiley, New York.

[7] Barrentine P (1993) *When the Canary Stops Singing* Berrett-Koehler, San Francisco.

[8] Kuhn T S (1962) *The Structure of Scientific Revolution* (2nd edn) University of Chicago Press, Chicago.

[9] Berger P L and Lockmann T (1966) *The Social Construction of Reality* New York, Doubleday.

[10] Kegan R (1994) *ibid*.

[11] Block P (1993) *Stewardship* Berrett-Koehler, San Francisco.

[12] Handy C (1989) *The Age of Unreason* Harvard Business School Press, Boston.

[13] Ackoff R (1994) *The Democratic Corporation* Oxford University Press, New York.

[14] Jung C (1963) *Memories, Dreams, Reflections Vintage Books*, New York, p.3.

[15] Lorde A (1984) *Sister Outsider* The Crossing Press, Freedom Ca; p.40.

3. Five Perspectives on Dialogue for Development

IN THIS CHAPTER: Each perspective approaches dialogue from different point of view; collectively these represent a richer and more complex understanding.

Contents

ORGANIZATIONAL LEARNING   *p. 21*

DEVELOPING SHARED MEANING   *p. 28*

CONDITIONS FOR RATIONAL DISCOURSE   *p. 34*

CO-OPERATION AND PRODUCTIVITY   *p. 39*

TRANSFORMATION   *p. 50*

 Sources   *p. 55*

3 Five Perspectives on Dialogue for Development

The five frameworks for dialogue reviewed here are based on the work of Chris Argyris,[1] David Bohm,[2] David Johnson and Roger Johnson,[3] Jack Mezirow,[4] and Paulo Freire.[5] Each approaches dialogue from a different discipline. But collectively, they afford the possibility of a richer and more complex understanding of a way to talk with each other than might be gained from only one perspective. You will certainly note differences among the five, as well as underlying commonalities. I invite you in reading through these to stay open to differing perspectives, to differentiate the concepts, and, at the end, to attempt with me to integrate the ideas into a meaningful whole.

ORGANIZATIONAL LEARNING

Limitations on learning

Chris Argyris has for twenty years been steadfast in his conviction that organizational members can learn to interact in ways that improve their own and their organization's learning. Through extensive data collection of some 6,000 cases, Argyris has found that organizational members consistently interact in ways that limit rather than facilitate their own learning. This "normal" way of interacting, which he has referred to as Model I, is characterized by such strategies as:

- asking questions in such a way as to get the other person to agree with one's own view;
- advocating one's own view in a manner that limits others' questioning of it; and
- privately evaluating the other person's view and attributing causes to it.

These and similar strategies are intended to persuade others to one's point of view, to minimize any negative feelings that may arise, and to appear rational and reasonable. Such goals do not seem inappropriate. It is, however, apparent how such strategies can limit learning. For example, if the questions I ask are designed to get the other person to agree with my own view, they will do little to elicit the other person's view. Thus, I will not learn how the other person reasons about the situation nor how the other's view may differ from my own. When I advocate my own view in a way that discourages others' questioning it, if my view is wrong, I will not be able to discover that. Likewise, when I privately evaluate the other's view and privately attribute cause to it, I cannot determine if my evaluation is accurate or if the attributions I make are correct. In other words, although each of these strategies may be effective in my "winning", they severely limit my learning.

Argyris has pointed out that people have a tendency to draw inferences very quickly from what they see and hear. This is done with such speed that they are often not aware that the conclusions they have reached are inferences, and moreover they quickly lose track of the data (what was said or done) that caused them to draw the inference. The ability to quickly draw inferences serves people well. It is a critical part of intelligence and effectiveness in functioning in a fast-paced world. But it also gets them into trouble. Because people tend to see their conclusions as "truth" or accurate, no effort is made to check them out - people make an hypothesis, sometimes on the basis of quite scanty data, and proceed to function on it as though it were true. For example, someone may infer that a frown means that the boss does not want to hear a different perspective, or that Fred's being late so many times means he is not very interested in the job, or that the group expects new members just to listen and not contribute.

Interaction practices

The set of interaction practices (Model II skills) that Argyris suggested are a way to overcome the negative consequences of the tendency to draw inferences quickly from scanty data include:

- actively inquiring into the other's views and the reasoning that supports them;
- advocating one's own view and reasoning in a way that encourages others to confront it and to help the speaker discover where the view may be mistaken;
- stating publicly the inferences that one makes about others and the data that leads to those inferences, and inviting others to correct the inferences if they are inaccurate.

Using such strategies, people may discover more adequate views than those they began with. With the help of others, individuals may also uncover assumptions that they were unaware of and which will afford them the opportunity to test whether those assumptions are valid.

As Argyris has pointed out many times, people require others to help them discover, invent, and especially produce new actions.

However, people will have to give up some of their goals in order to interact using Model II strategies. For example, a person will "win" using Model II strategies only if his or her reasoning and conclusions are in fact not fallacious. There is the risk of losing. There is the risk of being embarrassed if one's view is inaccurate, and the risk of embarrassing others if their reasoning does not support their views. When a person gives up the strategies that prevent others from expressing negative feelings, he or she risks having to experience those feelings.

Although Model II strategies are easily stated, they are very difficult to implement. They engage ingrained patterns for protecting oneself from embarrassment and threat. Those ingrained patterns automatically produce certain behaviours. For example, a person can ask "leading" questions and make inferences about other people without even realizing it; people may unwittingly design ways to state their views so that they cannot be tested, to prevent the embarrassment of discovering they are wrong.

Implementation

To become skilled at interacting using Model II strategies individuals must:

- identify the learning-limiting behaviours that they currently use;
- uncover the tacit assumptions that mediate those behaviours;
- alter those assumptions and design appropriate new behaviours; and

- practise those new behaviours until they become automatic.

The first and second steps are greatly facilitated by others. Because meaning structures often may be tacit and related automatic behaviour, they are difficult, if not impossible, to recognize in oneself. They are often, however, readily apparent to others.

For Model II skills to be developed, these steps must be engaged in repeatedly, as subsequent learning-limiting behaviours and tacit meaning structures are uncovered. To become skilful enough to use Model II skills in situations of even mild threat takes considerable time. Argyris has said up to a year before behaviour becomes automatic enough to use in situations of mild threat.

One way to facilitate the process of learning Model II skills is to ask a person to write about a difficult situation that he or she would have preferred to have handled better. The page is divided horizontally into two columns. In the right-hand column, the person records, as accurately as possible, the conversation that occurred in the course of the situation. In the left-hand column, the person records the thoughts and feelings that he or she had but did not express during the conversation. The case is then analysed by a group of colleagues who are also attempting to learn the Model II skill set. The case analysis is both an opportunity for the group to practice the Model II skills themselves and an opportunity to assist the case writer in identifying the ways that the person may have limited his or her own learning. See further Chapter 7.

Taken together the cases can provide useful insight into the defensive routines that limit the learning of the organization. Argyris[6] has also developed a corresponding interview process that is useful in collecting data related to defensive routines. The defensive routines are displayed in causal maps that can be confirmed or not confirmed by organizational stakeholders.

Argyris has acknowledged that Model II interaction is normative, not value-free. It is not a set of interaction skills that one could use as the means to achieve any given end. The normative end is, in fact, learning. The claim Argyris made for Model II skills is that the use of the skill set increases the amount of learning that results from the interaction. Learning, then, is the goal of Model II and its highest value.

Governing variables

There are values embedded within the three governing variables that Argyris articulates for Model II:

- valid information,
- free and informed choice, and
- internal commitment to the choice.

Valid information

When in conversation with others, people typically state their conclusions but less frequently offer the original data that led to those conclusions. In using the term "valid information", Argyris implied that people need to offer others both their *conclusions* and the *original data* that led them to those conclusions. Valid information gives others the opportunity to determine for themselves whether the data warrant the conclusion.

Valid information further requires that people make a concerted effort to gain directly observable data and reasoning from others. Then both parties have valid information. Finally, complete data must be offered, as opposed to withholding certain elements that might influence the other in ways the speaker would not prefer. Valid information requires that people make available to others all of the relevant data and that they report the data as accurately as they can. Underlying the idea of valid information is the scientific concept of a "community of inquiry guided by such norms as intersubjectively verifiable data, explicit inferences, and public falsifiability." [7]

Choice

The second and third governing variables - free and informed choice and internal commitment to that choice - are both based upon the first. For a choice to be informed, the individual must have all of the relevant information; for it to be free, the individual must not be coerced or make the choice out of fear or even because of the anticipation of extrinsic rewards. If someone agrees with another's opinion because he or she anticipates that the agreement will gain favour with that person, a free choice has not been made. A person makes a free and informed choice when the data support the choice, the logic is reasonable to him or her, and the choice is in concert with his or her own objectives and values. Internal commitment is a natural outgrowth of free and informed choice. People are most likely to be committed to those choices they make freely.

Summary: organizational learning

Purpose

To uncover one's own errors in reasoning and in so doing to uncover the defensive routines that prevent the organization, as a whole, from learning.

Process

Raise issues on-line in small groups or through left- and right-hand column written cases to uncover individuals' reasoning so they have the choice to alter them.

To create maps of the group's defensive routines for public discussion so that the group has the choice to alter them.

Skills and attitudes

Model II skills of advocacy and inquiry, publicly testing inferences, offering one's reasoning and seeking "disconfirmation".

Target audience

Both individuals and the organizations of which they are a part.

DEVELOPING SHARED MEANING

In contrast to Argyris' Model II idea, David Bohm's concept of dialogue is relatively technique-free. Despite this, the two ideas are surprisingly similar in terms of the goal toward which they strive: to uncover and examine the tacit theories-in-use (which Bohm referred to as "programmes") that mediate actions.

Bohm was a theoretical physicist, professor at the University of London, and a fellow of the Royal Society. His ideas of dialogue grew out of his experience and knowledge of physics; he described the world as an "unbroken flowing whole".[8] He provided compelling evidence from quantum physics for this view, contrasting it with the more mechanistic view of Newtonian physics and with the earlier Aristotelian view of the world as an integral organism. Yet Bohm acknowledged that quantum physics is also a "view" and, as with previous views, is ultimately based on a leap of faith. The starting point of any view is metaphysical, and only beyond that initial leap of faith is it based in logic or science. Thus he held his own view as a "programme" to be continually examined and questioned. He said, "We have to have enough faith in our world-view to work from it, but not that much faith that we think it's the final answer." [9]

According to Bohm, people typically deal with the world not as a whole but as though it were multiple fragments, one fragment being unrelated to others. His objection to a fragmentary view of the world was that it disposes people to think of the divisions between things as absolute and final rather than as having a limited utility and validity. Holding a fragmentary view, the person begins to act on the world as though it were indeed fragmented and in so doing creates a fragmented world that seems to exist independent of his or her actions. To use Argyris' term, people create a situation that is "self-sealing". A fragmentary view of the world is exemplified, for example, in viewing the boundaries of countries as authentic or manifest. Such a view makes it possible to see the people of France and Germany as two entities rather than people divided by an arbitrarily drawn line, a line that, given different conditions, might be placed very differently. When the mechanistic explanation of reality is taken to its ultimate implication, people are left with a universe which is basically indifferent to humankind and in which there is meaning only to the extent that individuals can construct meaning in their own eyes. It is this fragmentary view of the world that Bohm hoped to overcome through dialogue.

Society, to work, must be based on shared meaning, which Bohm likened to the cement that holds society together. At present, society has an incoherent set of meanings, a poor quality cement, so it is falling apart. His goal, then, was to develop not higher individual intelligence but higher social intelligence. The first task in creating such shared meanings is simply to apprehend the meanings of others. That, in and of itself, will bring a certain order. Bohm said that dialogue is a way to apprehend the meaning of others and to thereby experience the wholeness of the world rather than the fragments into which understanding is broken.

Dialogue and discussion

Bohm contrasted dialogue with discussion.[10] "Dialogue" comes from the Greek word *dialogos*, meaning "through"; dialogue is like a stream running between two banks. He noted that it is the stream that counts. The banks merely give form to the stream. The stream is analogous to the free flow of meaning between people. "Discussion", on the other hand, has the same root word as percussion or concussion, meaning "to break things apart or to analyse". Discussion leads to separate points of view. Dialogue leads to shared meaning.

"Programmes"

Bohm referred to the products of thinking as "programmes". People are unaware of these programmes, not of their content but of their nature. The programmes people construct appear to them to be in some sense reality or truth. Bohm pointed out that thinking (the production of programmes) is a slow process whereas the recall and use of programmes is swift. Thinking cannot keep up with thought (programmes). Thus the programmes that people have constructed cannot be changed through thinking alone.

Bohm compared these programmes to the bright lights of Las Vegas. The lights, in their nearness, prevent people from knowing or seeing the stars beyond the lights. The lights constitute reality, blotting out the larger universe. If the lights are "dissolved," then the stars appear and that new reality is apparent. Bohm suggested that dialogue is a way to uncover and "dissolve" programmes.

Conditions for productive dialogue

Concerns about the pervasiveness of programmes made Bohm unwilling even to specify the conditions of productive dialogue, seeing such conditions themselves as "programmes" that have to be examined. According to him,

> *"One of the difficulties is that the thoughts contain all sorts of presuppositions which limit us and hold us in rigid grooves. What we have to do is discover these presuppositions and get rid of them - get free of them. I don't think that we can establish conditions for a dialogue, except to say that we both want to make a dialogue."* [11]

31

His guidance for dialogue, then, is minimal. To create a dialogue requires a group that will meet without purpose or a specified goal so that its members can talk freely. The group needs to be large enough that subcultures can develop within it. In a small group, Bohm said, people can hide their deeper ideas through politeness and avoidance. In a large group, of twenty or thirty people, sub-groups will form and raise the deeper issues. But he noted that, as soon as people try to talk about things that are of such importance, they get excited and stop hearing each other.

Bohm proposed that participants in dialogue suspend their assumptions - that is, that they consider what both their and others' assumptions mean without judging or attempting to come to any compromise. When all the participants in a group agree to suspend their assumptions and attempt to apprehend the meanings of others, they are already in the act of sharing meaning. Bohm said it is not necessary that everyone hold the same opinions for shared meaning to emerge, that the joint agreement to apprehend the meaning of others is more important than the content of the opinions and assumptions themselves. "When you listen to somebody else, whether you like it or not, what they say becomes part of you."[12] So in a dialogue everybody's ideas are held by all. There is a common pool of information. Out of this social intelligence comes something new.

It is holding on to assumptions and defending them that get in the way of dialogue. He eschewed persuasion and attempts to convince others, maintaining that if something is right there is no need for persuasion. "Truth," said Bohm, "does not emerge from opinions; it must emerge from something else - perhaps from a more free movement of this tacit mind." [13]

Bohm suggested that dialogue be an exchange that is

conducted without an agenda and without a leader. He used the analogy of an empty space in which anything may come in. In describing dialogue, Bohm related a story about a North American Indian tribe of hunter-gatherers. From time to time the whole tribe would come together in a circle and talk. No one appeared to have called the meeting or to have led it; the group made no decisions and seemingly had no agenda. Yet when the meeting ended people knew what to do because they now understood each other. They might then get together in small groups and make plans or decide to do something.

Conclusion

Bohm realized that dialogue is not easy. It is difficult to hear an assumption that contradicts one's own; it is difficult to see some people dominating the dialogue while others say nothing. As with Argyris' Model II skills, a certain vulnerability is demanded.

> *"An idea must be vulnerable - you have to be ready to drop it, just as the person who holds the idea must be vulnerable, I think. He should not identify with it."* [14]

Summary: developing shared meaning

Purpose

To develop "social intelligence".

To create the shared understanding (glue) that might better hold together our fragmented society.

Process

Minimally structured dialogue in large groups of 20 or

more that meet over several months. Groups are facilitated only initially.

Skills and attitudes

Willingness to suspend one's own assumptions while reflecting on the ideas, feelings, and actions of the group.

Target Audience

Society as a whole.

CONDITIONS FOR RATIONAL DISCOURSE

Jack Mezirow has described himself as an adult educator, coming out of the emancipatory tradition of Paulo Freire and Saul Alinsky. His hope is that, through learning and reflection, adults can free themselves of what William Blake in his poem, *London*, called "mind-forg'd manacles". As did Argyris and Bohm, Mezirow has pointed out the need for adults to help each other uncover their tacit assumptions. Mezirow's focus has been more individual than the other theorists. I include his concepts here because he has provided clear guidance about the conditions under which dialogue can occur and because he has differentiated that which can be validated through proof from that which must rely on dialogue for validation.

Types of learning

Drawing heavily on the work of Jurgen Habermas, Mezirow [15] framed three kinds of learning, one of which, "communicative" learning, requires interaction with others of the type discussed above. It will be helpful first to differentiate the three types and then to explain why communicative learning requires dialogue.

Instrumental learning

The most familiar type of learning described by Mezirow is "instrumental" - that is, learning that leads to the control and manipulation of the environment, which in this definition includes other people. Instrumental learning is based on empirical knowledge and involves predictions about observable events. It involves cause-and-effect relationships that can be proven or disproved. Testing hypotheses that lead to greater control over situations produces knowledge. Quality control is an application of instrumental learning.

Communicative learning

Communicative learning is associated with the practical rather than the empirical. It is learning to understand what others mean and to make oneself understood. The goal of communicative learning is to gain insight and to reach common understanding rather than to control. Most of the problems and issues people deal with in organizations fall into this category, including intentions, social concepts, politics, reasons, feelings, and beliefs.

Using communicative learning, one cannot "prove" something with empirical evidence. It cannot, for example, be proven that Jones would be the best person to fill the vice-president slot or that a report has sufficient depth to satisfy a client's needs. According to Mezirow,

> *"We are continually confronted with having to determine the validity of reports, predictions, explanations, arguments, and denials as well as the implicit claims of validity involved in justifying commands, requests, excuses, and recommendations."* [16]

With communicative learning, validity can be determined in one of two ways. The first is to rely on force, tradition, or authority, as in a religious dogma or the divine right of kings. The second way is to rely on a broad consensus of those who are informed, rational, and objective. But even here the idea is not one of simply voting but rather an opinion that is reached through a deliberation in which each person has the opportunity to hear, influence, and challenge others. Consensual validation is based on the assumption that any unbiased group that had available to them the same information would arrive at a similar conclusion. It is the assumption at the heart of the Enlightenment: that the human mind is capable of using logic and reason to understand the world rather than having to rely on the interpretation of someone who claims authority through force, tradition, or divine right.

Consensual validation is recognizable as the process employed in a jury of peers. A group of objective individuals reviews the evidence and arguments and renders a decision, which, hopefully, is the same as another jury would render hearing the same evidence. Although less formalized in most situations, the same principles apply. People believe something is valid if, after examining the available data, a group of reasonable individuals comes to a consensus.

Because consensus may also be reached through coercion, it is necessary to construct standards related to objectivity. According to Mezirow, those include:[17]

- having accurate and complete information;
- being free from coercion and distorting self-deception;
- being able to weigh evidence and assess arguments objectively;

- being open to alternative perspectives;
- being able to become critically reflective upon presuppositions and their consequences;
- having equal opportunity to participate (including the chance to challenge, question, refute, and reflect and to hear others do the same);
- being able to accept an informed, objective, and rational consensus as a legitimate test of validity.

Emancipatory learning

The third type of learning is "emancipatory." The goal of emancipatory learning is to identify and reflect on distorted meaning perspectives. Mezirow has pointed out, as did Bohm (in his view of programmes), that individuals understand the world through a frame that they have constructed and that frame is often distorted by institutional, linguistic, and environmental forces that have been taken for granted by the individual. An example might be that women cannot succeed in upper management or that wealthy people should have greater protection under the law than the poor. Emancipatory learning is achieved through critical self-reflection but, as with Bohm's concept of dissolving programmes, requires others to provide perspective.

Conclusion

It is Mezirow's concern that people have taken instrumental learning as the model for all learning and that they fail to understand that only instrumental learning can be validated through empirical means. For all other learning people must rely on each other and on establishing conditions that assist their ability to think together rationally.

Mezirow has focused on the individual and the ways institutions including government, corporations, and educational organizations impart distorting assumptions to the individual. His goal has been to free the individual of such assumptions through critical reflection; to do that he or she must also make institutions aware of their tacit assumptions.

Summary: conditions for rational discourse

Purpose

To free individuals of the distorting assumptions imparted through institutions, including government, corporations, and education.

Process

Deliberate on a topic to achieve a broad consensus of those who are informed, rational, and objective.

Skills and attitudes

Be able to weigh evidence and assess arguments objectively.

Be open to alternative perspectives.

Be able to reflect critically on presuppositions and their consequences.

Accept informed, objective, and rational consensus as a legitimate test of validity.

Target audience

Individuals and the institutions with which they interact that unknowingly impart distorted assumptions.

CO-OPERATION AND PRODUCTIVITY

David Johnson and Roger Johnson are the foremost researchers on the relationship among learning, co-operation and productivity. They have based their work on Morton Deutsch's theory of social interdependence[18]. Over the last twenty years they have conducted more than forty studies to understand the conditions for and the outcomes of co-operation, particularly as it relates to learning. In addition they have conducted a meta-analysis of a hundred years of research with over five hundred studies related to this topic. Much of Johnson and Johnson's own work has been conducted in educational settings, although confirmation of their findings has involved all sectors. The conclusions presented here are primarily drawn from their meta-analysis.

There are three ways individuals can take action: co-operatively, competitively, and independently. Through co-operative action, individuals promote the success of others; through competitive action, they obstruct the success of others; independent action has no affect on others' success. Each of these three types of action can be understood as forms of social interdependence.

Benefits

Although Johnson and Johnson have said much about all three conditions, I will limit my discussion to their findings on co-operation, because it is that situation in which dialogue is critical. Four benefits of co-operative action are supported in their meta-analysis: productivity, reasoning strategies, process gain, and transfer of learning.

Productivity

In the more than 185 studies that have compared the impact of co-operative and competitive situations on achievement, the evidence is overwhelming that greater productivity is attained through co-operation. When co-operative situations are contrasted with individualistic situations (226 studies), the results are similar. These findings hold for both individual achievement and a total group's achievement.

Reasoning strategies

A second benefit is the improved quality of reasoning strategies that individuals employ in a co-operative situation. Reasoning strategies include, for example, integrating new information with prior knowledge, identifying concepts underlying data, problem solving, and metaphoric reasoning. The use of such strategies is increased in co-operative situations as well as the quality of the strategies themselves. In addition, "metacognition", or knowledge about one's thinking processes, is more frequently in evidence in co-operative situations than it is in competitive or independent situations. Metacognition is critical because it leads to the generalized improvement in learning capability.

Process gain

A third benefit is process gain - that is, in co-operative situations, new ideas or solutions are generated which would not have occurred if individuals were working independently. Again, there is significantly more process gain through co-operative situations than either competitive or independent situations.

Transfer of learning

The final benefit noted in this meta-analysis is transfer of learning. By "transfer of learning", Johnson and Johnson meant what an individual learned in the group situation that he or she is able to use in other circumstances, ones that no longer involve the original group. The transfer finding is most significant when the knowledge gained is at a higher rather than lower cognitive level. With low-level cognitive knowledge, there is little difference in whether the learning took place independently, competitively, or co-operatively. However, with more complex understandings, co-operative situations produce greater transfer.

Conditions for positive outcomes

These four findings, drawn from hundreds of studies, provide strong evidence that co-operative situations produce greater learning and achievement than do competitive or independent situations. Not all co-operation is effective, however, as anyone who has participated in a group situation can attest. The benefits described above do not occur by simply putting organizational members in a group and instructing them to reach a given outcome.

There are a number of ways in which such benefits

may be derailed in a group situation. For example, some members may do less than their share of the work, a "free-rider" effect; members who are viewed as having greater expertise or authority may be deferred to; and groups may create dysfunctional divisions of labour and certain individuals may dominate the interaction. Thus, it is only under certain conditions that co-operative efforts achieve the beneficial outcomes: (1) positive interdependence, (2) social skills, and (3) promotive interaction. It is the third of these that requires dialogue. Before discussing promotive interaction, I must frame that critical factor in terms of the other two.

Positive interdependence

Positive interdependence implies that individuals are linked with others in a way that one cannot achieve without others achieving as well. Moreover, in order to achieve the outcome, each individual must co-ordinate his or her activities with others. Simply being a member of a group does not automatically lead to higher levels of achievement, nor does group discussion alone, nor does a mere exchange of information; there must also be positive interdependence. For positive interdependence to exist, all individuals must be oriented toward an outcome (outcome interdependence) and the means through which that outcome is reached - such as resources, roles, and tasks - must be interdependent (means interdependence) as well.

Social skills

Co-operation requires individuals who are skilled in interpersonal and small-group interaction. Such skills might include conflict resolution, communication, trust building, and decision making, to name a few. The group must periodically reflect on how well it is interacting and on what it might do to improve the way the group is functioning. It is clear, however, that social skills in the absence of positive interdependence and "promotive" interaction do not increase productivity and achievement.

"Promotive" interaction

Johnson and Johnson defined promotive interaction as "individuals encouraging and facilitating each other's efforts to achieve, complete tasks, and produce in order to reach the group's goals". The interaction is described as "face to face" and although electronic or other technologically mediated interaction may produce the same results, that has not been tested through these studies.

All three of the conditions of co-operation are necessary for increased productivity and achievement. However, of the three, promotive interaction is clearly the most critical. Johnson and Johnson described nine elements of promotive interaction:[19]

- Providing each other with efficient and effective help and assistance;
- Exchanging needed resources such as information and materials and processing information more efficiently and effectively;
- Providing each other with feedback in order to improve subsequent performance of assigned tasks and responsibilities;
- Challenging each other's conclusions and reasoning in order to promote higher-quality decision making and greater insight into the problems being considered;
- Advocating the exertion of effort to achieve mutual goals;

- Influencing each other's efforts to achieve the group's goals;
- Acting in trusting and trustworthy ways;
- Being motivated to strive for mutual benefit; and
- Having a moderate level of arousal characterized by low anxiety and stress.

Many of these elements are self-explanatory. However, it is useful to expand on some of these.

Information exchange and cognitive processes

Individuals exchange their data, conclusions, reasoning, and questions with others in promotive interaction. Although the cognitive benefits to the receiver of such an exchange are apparent, there is evidence that it is the speaker who makes the greatest cognitive gains from the exchange. Recent studies have shown that the act of orally summarizing information works to strengthen the speaker's understanding of that information. Such a finding would seem to bear out the insight of the Roman philosopher who said "Qui docet descit" (Whoever teaches, learns twice). Individuals organize information differently if they are going to present it to others than if they are trying to understand it solely for their own use. It is in the act of speaking that people tend to organize cognitively what they know.

A second beneficial action to the speaker is "perspective-taking" - that is, the act of paraphrasing the ideas and arguments of others. Perspective taking is more than just being able to play back others' argument in order to check with them for accuracy. It is the ability to comprehend and voice how the situation appears from another's standpoint. Perspective taking is the opposite of egocentrism - in which the individual is locked into a single view of the situation and is unaware of the limitations of that view or that other viable views may exist.

When one voices the perspective of another, that action inclines the other to disclose information more fully than if the perspective were not voiced. The additional information and the fuller comprehension of another perspective both work to increase the development of new knowledge on a complex issue. It is necessary, however, to hold both one's own and others' perspectives in mind at the same time to create new knowledge. Simply listening to another's perspective is less facilitative of the creation of new knowledge than is the actual voicing of the other's perspective. People place such a high value on information that it is almost counter-intuitive to realize that the amount of actual information within a group is less important in reaching a high-quality solution to a problem than is actually voicing others' perspectives.

Having placed the emphasis here on the speaker rather than on the receiver of information, I should at least acknowledge that the receiver also benefits cognitively. In particular, the receiver is able to incorporate the knowledge, skills, and reasoning of others into his or her own understanding.

Controversy

When promotive interaction occurs, an unavoidable outcome is controversy. When managed constructively, controversy promotes uncertainty about one's own views, which leads to an active search for information, resulting in the re-organization of one's understanding. The constructive, rather than a destructive, management of controversy depends upon the group's social skills.

Controversy, as the term is used here,

"exists when one person's ideas, information, conclusions, theories, and opinions are incompatible with those of another, and the two seek to reach agreement."[20]

Embedded within this definition are positive outcome and means interdependence. The outcome inter-dependence is the hoped for agreement and the means interdependence is different information. The process through which controversy leads to increased productivity is as follows:[21]

1 When individuals are presented with a problem or decision, they hold an initial conclusion based on categorizing and organizing incomplete information, their limited experiences, and their specific perspectives.

2 As each individual presents his or her conclusion and its rationale to others, the person engages in cognitive rehearsal, deepening the understanding of his or her position, and discovers higher-level reasoning strategies.

3 When other people confront the person with different conclusions based on their information, experiences, and perspectives, he or she becomes uncertain as to the correctness of his or her views. A state of conceptual conflict or disequilibrium is created.

4 Uncertainty, conceptual conflict, and disequilibrium motivate an active search for more information, new experiences, and a more adequate cognitive perspective and reasoning process in hopes of resolving the uncertainty.

5 As the person adapts his or her cognitive perspectives and reasoning through understanding and accommodating the perspectives and

reasoning of others, a new, re-conceptualized, and re-organized conclusion is derived. Novel solutions and decisions that, on balance, are qualitatively better are detected.

Johnson and Johnson differentiated controversy from concurrence-seeking, which they defined as a process in which group members inhibit disagreement or the critique of an opposing position in order to reach agreement. In controversy, there must be both co-operation and conflict. The conditions under which productivity is increased through controversy are as follows:

1 A co-operative goal structure exists through which information is accurately communicated. Controversy is designed as win-win. So individuals:
   • feel safe enough to challenge each other's ideas;
   • value controversy rather than viewing it as a shortcoming;
   • are willing to deal with feelings as well as ideas and information; and
   • recognize similarities in ideas as well as differences.

2 There is heterogeneity of members. The greater the heterogeneity, the greater the amount of time members spend in controversy, thus the greater the productivity. Heterogeneity can exist in information, ability, reasoning strategies, and personality, as well as the more acknowledged differences of sex, race, background, and age.

3 Relevant information is distributed among members. ("Relevant" in this case means related to the task the group is working on.) If one individual has all of the information, or if no one

has relevant information, productivity will not be increased. However, the more information the group has distributed among its members the more productive the group will be.

4 Members have the ability to disagree with each other without creating defensiveness. This condition is directly related to individuals' social skills. Two skills in particular are needed:

- the ability "to disagree with each other's ideas while confirming each other's personal competence." [22]
- the ability to take the perspective of the other, which was discussed above.

5 Members have the ability to engage in rational argument. Engaging in rational argument implies that members keep an open mind, are willing to be influenced by the cogent arguments of others, are able to use logical reasoning and to determine when reasoning leads to valid conclusions, are themselves able to organize their reasoning to present to others, and so on.

When these conditions are present, controversy produces increased productivity and achievement over concurrence-seeking groups, competitive debate, or individuals working alone.

Conclusion

A final and hopeful note should be added to this discussion of Johnson and Johnson's work. They described a spiral in which trust is needed to achieve co-operation, but co-operation also leads to increased trust, which in turn leads to increased co-operation. In fact, the research shows that people seek out those with whom they have acted co-operatively, to again engage in co-operative action. Given the high correlation between co-operation and productivity, the spiral of co-operation may also be a spiral of productivity.

Summary: co-operation and productivity

Purpose

To increase the learning and the concomitant productivity in groups.

Process

Promotive interaction: face-to-face interaction in which individuals encourage each other to achieve, complete tasks, and produce in order to reach the group's goals.

Skills and attitudes

Provide each other with effective help and feedback.

Exchange needed resources.

Challenge each other's conclusions and reasoning.

Act in trusting and trustworthy ways.

Advocate an exertion of effort to achieve mutual goals.

Be motivated to strive for mutual benefit.

Have a moderate level of arousal.

Target audience

Groups who need to learn with and from each other, such as teams, class members, study groups.

TRANSFORMATION

Paulo Freire is a Brazilian educator whose life-long work has been the education of illiterate adults in the Third World, both through his own practice and through the development of theory that has influenced educators worldwide. The antecedents of his theoretical ideas can be found in the thinking of Jean-Paul Sartre, Erich Fromm, Jose Ortega y Gasset, Mao Tse-tung, Martin Luther King, and Che Guevara. These thinkers, coupled with his own remarkable socio-political insights, led him not only to understand the political potency of bringing literacy to the disenfranchised but also to advocate for the legitimate right of all people to participate in creating their own culture and world. His work with illiterate peasants in Brazil so threatened the existing order that he was jailed and subsequently exiled. Much of his work in Latin America has been through UNESCO and the Chilean Institute for Agrarian Reform. Freire was himself born into poverty and experienced firsthand the disenfranchisement of the poor and oppressed.

For Freire dialogue is the process through which human beings collectively transform their world. That transformation involves altering their taken-for-granted assumptions about their world and their relationship to it. This transformation is not conceived of as a one-time change - that is, as a change from an incorrect position to a more correct one - but rather as integral to human development. It is the process of evolving new meaning as humans interact with their world in ways that change the world and are in turn changed by it. "To exist humanly, is to *name* the world, to change it." [23] Dialogue, then, is a creative process, one in which meaning is created or re-created.

It is also a social process. Although meaning is constructed in the minds of individuals, it is through dialogue - the process of communicating, challenging, and affirming meaning - that the world is transformed. Naming the world, transforming it, is the way humans find significance, thus it is an "existential necessity". As such, it cannot be the privilege of an elite few but rather is the right of everyone. For this reason, the naming cannot be done alone, nor for others, for that robs them of their words.

Freire's use of the term "naming" is appropriate. To give a name to something, whether that something is a concrete object, a newly conceived concept, or an action, is a way of making it available for dialogue. As long as the "something" is taken for granted it is not available for dialogue. Likewise, renaming allows people to see a familiar something in a new way. Thus in proposing that all people have the right to participate in naming of the world, Freire is talking about the power to re-conceptualize the world, to think in new ways about it.

Dialogue, according to Freire, is about both reflection and action: "To speak a true word is to transform the world." [24] By transforming the world Freire means to alter it in ways that allow people to be more human. His emphasis in this quotation is, however, on the term "true". True words, spoken in dialogue with others, alter the world. This action and reflection occur simultaneously, not sequentially. In fact, Freire did not dichotomize acting and reflecting; together they are praxis.

Dialogue is also, according to Freire, not a technique used to help achieve some preferred result. Rather it is part of the historical progress of human beings becoming more human, more aware, and more conscious. However, for Freire, as for the other theorists I have discussed above, dialogue is not just talk. The term is reserved for a way of interacting that is truer, more open, and more human.

Freire often referred to the "non-dialogic man", individuals who attempt to indoctrinate others, requiring them to adjust to a reality that is already defined.

Rational perspective

What does dialogue require of people? Those who engage in dialogue must come to it with humility, love, faith, and hope - a formidable list of characteristics, but one that exemplifies a relational perspective, rather than technique.

Humility

Freire wrote eloquently about the need for humility in this passage from *Pedagogy of the Oppressed*.

> "Dialogue cannot exist without humility. The naming of the world, through which people constantly re-create that world, cannot be an act of arrogance. Dialogue, as the encounter of those addressed to the common task of learning and acting, is broken if the parties (or one of them) lack humility. How can I dialogue if I always project ignorance onto others and never perceive my own? How can I dialogue if I regard myself as a case apart from others - mere "its" in whom I cannot recognize other "I"s? How can I dialogue if I consider myself a member of the in-group of "pure" men, the owners of truth and knowledge, for whom all non-members are "these people" or "the great unwashed"? . . . Someone who cannot acknowledge himself to be as mortal as everyone else still has a long way to go before he can reach the point of encounter. At the point

> *of encounter there are neither utter ignoramuses nor*
> *perfect sages; there are only people who are attempting,*
> *together, to learn more than they now know."* [25]

Love

Freire wrote about dialogue as the creation and re-creation of meaning and suggests that creation is an act of love. Thus dialogue cannot exist in the absence of love of the world and of humankind. "Love is at the same time the foundation of dialogue and dialogue itself." [26]

Faith

In addition to humility and love, those who engage in dialogue need faith in the ability of people to make and remake their world. This is not faith in an elite group who have shown some particular aptitude, nor faith in the well-educated who have developed a certain expertise, but rather faith in the ability of average human beings to comprehend their world and, with others, to transform their world. Freire said,

> *"Faith in man[kind] is an a priori requirement for*
> *dialogue; the 'dialogical man' believes in other men*
> *even before he meets them face to face. . . . Without*
> *this faith in man, dialogue is a farce which inevitably*
> *degenerates into paternalistic manipulation."* [27]

Hope

Freire said that dialogue requires hope. Without hope that things can change there is no need for dialogue. Hopelessness begets silence, not dialogue. If individuals do not expect anything to happen as a result of their dialogue, the dialogue will be empty and meaningless.

Critical thinking

Finally, dialogue requires individuals to engage in critical thinking. Freire differentiates critical thinking from naive thinking. Naive thinking sees the future as extrapolation from the past. The naive thinker's focus is on accommodation to the anticipated future, which is seen as inevitable. The critic, by contrast, is focused on the continued transformation of reality.

Summary: transformation

Purpose

To free groups and individuals from the tacit assumptions that keep them oppressed.

Process

Talk together in equal relationship without differentiated teaching and learning roles.

Skills and attitudes

Humility, love, faith, hope and critical thinking.

Target audience

Populations that are oppressed by cultural norms and political processes.

SOURCES FOR CHAPTER 3

1 Argyris C (1990) *Overcoming Organizational Defenses: facilitating organizational learning* Allyn & Bacon, Boston; Argyris C (1992) *On Organizational Learning* Blackwell, Cambridge Ma; Argyris C (1993) *Knowledge for Action* Jossey-Bass, San Francisco; Argyris C, Putman R and Smith D M (1985) Action Science Jossey-Bass, San Francisco.
2 Bohm D (1985) *Unfolding Meaning: a weekend of dialogue with David Bohm* Ark Paperbacks, New York; Bohm D (1990) On Dialogue (translation) David Bohm Seminars, Ojai Ca.
3 Johnson D W and Johnson R T (1989) *Co-operation and Competition: theory and research* Interaction Book Company, Edina Mn.
4 Mezirow J (1991) *Transformative Dimensions of Adult Learning* Jossey-Bass, San Francisco.
5 Freire P (1970) *Pedagogy of the Oppressed* Seabury Press, New York; Freire P (1994) *Pedagogy of the Oppressed* (rev. edn) Continuum Publishing, New York.
6 Argyris C (1993) *Knowledge for Action* Jossey-Bass, San Francisco.
7 Argyris C et al (1985) *ibid*.
8 Bohm D (1985) *ibid*.
9 Bohm D (1985) *ibid*, p.4.
10 Bohm D (1990) *ibid*.
11 Bohm D (1985) *ibid*, p.37.
12 Bohm D (1992) *ibid*, p.119.
13 Bohm D (1990) *ibid*, p.22.
14 Bohm D (1985) *ibid*, p.40.
15 Mezirow J (1991) *ibid*.
16 Mezirow J (1991) *ibid*, p.76.
17 Mezirow J (1991) *ibid*, pp.77-78.
18 Deutsch M (1949) "An Experimental Study of the Effects of Co-operation and Competition upon Group Process" *Human Relations* 2, 199-231.
19 Johnson D W and Johnson R T (1989) *ibid*, p.63.
20 Johnson D W and Johnson R T (1989) *ibid*, p.87.
21 Adapted from Johnson D W and Johnson R T (1989) *ibid*, pp 91-92.
22 Johnson D W and Johnson R T (1989) *ibid*, p.102.
23 Freire P (1970) *ibid*, p.76
24 Freire P (1970) *ibid*, p.75.
25 Freire P (1994) *ibid*, p.71.
26 Freire P (1970) *ibid*, pp.77-78.
27 Freire P (1970) ibid, p.79.

4. Practical Observations on Dialogue

IN THIS CHAPTER: A synthesis of the five perspectives on dialogue that represents my own view, which is informed by the thinkers discussed in chapter 3 but which is not limited to their ideas.

Contents

A DEFINITION OF DIALOGUE   *p. 59*

THE PURPOSE OF DIALOGUE   *p. 60*

THE ROLE OF OTHERS IN LEARNING   *p. 61*

PEOPLE ALREADY KNOW HOW TO
    HAVE A DIALOGUE   *p. 62*

DIALOGUE IS A RELATIONSHIP   *p. 63*

DIALOGUE CAN OFFSET THE INSTRUMENTAL
    NATURE OF WORK RELATIONSHIPS   *p. 64*

DIALOGUE AFFIRMS THE INTELLECTUAL
    CAPACITY OF ORDINARY HUMAN BEINGS   *p. 66*

THE OUTCOME OF DIALOGUE IS UNPREDICTABLE   *p. 67*

DIALOGUE IS PARADOXICAL   *p. 68*

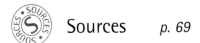

Sources   *p. 69*

4 Practical Observations on Dialogue

Coming as they do from different disciplines, the theorists discussed above offer remarkably similar ideas about dialogue. Although some include ideas that the others do not, and there are clear differences among them, none basically contradicts the others. The observations that I offer in this chapter are, in one sense, a summary of these theorists; in another sense, they represent my own view of dialogue, which has been informed by these thinkers but which is not limited to their ideas.

A DEFINITION OF DIALOGUE

In my view, dialogue is talk - a special kind of talk - that affirms the person-to-person relationship between discussants and which acknowledges their collective right and intellectual capacity to make sense of the world. Therefore, it is not talk that is "one way", such as a sales pitch, a directive, or a lecture; rather it involves mutuality and "jointness". I do not want to suggest that dialogue is without emotion and passion or that it is without confrontation and challenge. It involves both, but within bounds that affirm the legitimacy of others' perspectives.

Dialogue has the potential to alter the meaning each individual holds and, by so doing, is capable of transforming the group, organization, and society. The relationship between the individual and the collective is reciprocal and is mediated through talk. People are both recipients of tacit assumptions and the creators of them. In this way dialogue results in the co-creation of meaning. The meaning that is created is shared across group members; a common understanding is developed. I am hesitant here to use the familiar word "consensus", because it seems too restricted, limited to a decision-making process. I mean something more encompassing. The common understanding engendered by dialogue is one in which each individual has internalized the perspectives of the others and thus is enriched by a sense of the whole. Dialogue brings people to a new way of perceiving an issue that may be of concern to all. That new understanding might include what actions (decisions) should be taken individually and collectively, but such resulting actions are not its essence; its essence is that people have collectively constructed new meaning.

THE PURPOSE OF DIALOGUE

It is worthwhile to consider what purpose dialogue can serve. Argyris has defined the goal as uncovering one's own and the organization's unintentional errors that limit learning. Mezirow's goal has been emancipating individuals from the untested assumptions that limit their development as human beings. Johnson and Johnson took as their goal learning and productivity. The goal Bohm had in mind was shared meaning, which he believed people could come to by dissolving the programmes that blind them. Finally, Freire's goal has been to transform the world through understanding and re-creating it. In all of these perspectives there is the intent to uncover that which is tacit - to become aware of the paradigm in which those individuals engaged in the dialogue are themselves embedded. By making manifest that which has been taken for granted, the participants in the dialogue are able to hold their assumptions up for examination and, when warranted, to construct new joint meaning that is tested against their reasoning.

THE ROLE OF OTHERS IN LEARNING

Dialogue occurs in a group setting. The group may be quite small, as in some of Argyris' and perhaps Johnson and Johnson's groups, but it is clear that Bohm and Freire were talking about larger groups, even forty or more. People often mistakenly think the prefix *dia* means two and thus think of a dialogue as only occurring between two people. But in its Greek origin *dia* means "passing through," as in diathermy, or "thoroughly" or "completely," as in diagnosis. Thus, dialogue is a social event, a community of people thinking together.

As each of these theorists has suggested, people need others to see what they cannot see for themselves. That is a difficult idea in a society steeped in individualism. To acknowledge that others are needed is the act of humility that Freire talked about or the acceptance of our vulnerability that Bohm referenced. People seem more comfortable with the idea that others can provide them with new information than with the idea that they need others to put their own thinking to a test. Stephen Brookfield has said,

> *"Trying to understand the motive for our actions or*
> *attempting to identify the assumptions undergirding*

*our apparently objective, rational beliefs is like trying
to catch our psychological tail. . . . We must hold our
behaviour up for scrutiny by others, and in their
interpretation of our actions we are given a reflection,
a mirroring of our own actions from an unfamiliar
psychological vantage point."* [1]

PEOPLE ALREADY KNOW HOW TO HAVE DIALOGUE

Dialogue need not be thought of as something unfamiliar
or new. People already have the necessary skills. For
example, most people can think of someone with whom
they engage in a certain kind of conversation on a
consistent basis - perhaps a long-time colleague, a
cherished friend, or a spouse. These are conversations in
which each person works hard to grasp the perspective of
the other, sensing that he or she is not being judgmental
but rather trying to see the world through the other's
eyes. Each person has his or her thinking seriously
challenged and seriously supported. This is dialogue, and
although it may not always feel comfortable nor be
satisfying in the moment, it is authentic in a way most
work conversations are not. If people value such talk, it is
in part because they value the individual with whom it
takes place and recognize the value that that person places
on them. People value the content of the dialogue as well,
recognizing that they have grown and changed through it.

If one accepts this hypothesis, that people are capable
of engaging in a dialogue without necessarily having to
learn new skills or technique, then dialogue is more about
the nature of the relationship between people than about
the specific words they say or the technique they employ.
See further, Chapter 7.

DIALOGUE IS A RELATIONSHIP

When people talk with others they convey not only a content message but also who the others are in relation to themselves - for instance, that the others are equal, less knowledgeable, revered, or unimportant. That relationship is conveyed through what is said and what is withheld, the choice of words, tone, and non-verbal actions. The relationship expressed through dialogue is one in which the other is valued, trusted, and an equal whose ideas are respected if not always agreed with. People are in a person-to-person relationship with the other.

Freire's five requirements for dialogue cited above - humility, love, faith, hope, and critical thinking - are about the nature of the relationship between the speaker and those with whom the speaker is in dialogue. When Freire said, "Self-sufficiency is incompatible with dialogue. Men and women who lack humility (or have lost it) cannot come to the people, cannot be their partners in naming the world",[2] he was talking about how people view themselves in relationship to others.

Even in Argyris' more technical approach to dialogue, at the heart of Model II skills, there are the values of valid information, free and informed choice, and internal commitment to the choice. Argyris' values speak to the nature of the relationship between people - that is, that the intent of the individual should not be to use others, either purposefully or unwittingly, but rather to guard free and informed choice for either him- or herself and others.

I am suggesting here that dialogue is not a difference in technique but a difference in relationship. I seriously question whether more technique is necessary. There is already a great deal of technique that relates to clear feedback, supportive and clarifying statements, air time, paraphrasing to check out what is understood, and so on. That is not to say that people consistently make use of the technique that is available to them. But even when they do, they may not change their intent to manipulate or control. People may have altered their words but not the nature of their relationship to others.

Dialogue transpires in the context of relationship, and central to it is the idea that through interaction people acknowledge the wholeness, not just the utility, of others.

DIALOGUE CAN OFFSET THE INSTRUMENTAL NATURE OF WORK RELATIONSHIPS

The relationship built into much of the talk at work is instrumental - that is, the person with whom one is talking is viewed as a means to accomplish an objective. The term "human resource", used as a synonym for organizational members, symbolizes the instrumental nature of relationships in organizations. To speak of people as a "resource" is to relegate them to the status of objects, comparable to equipment or supplies. The use of the term makes it possible to deny that the resource, the persons involved, are human beings with purposes and wills of their own. Even the term "employee" carries with it an instrumental flavour.

When Bohm eschewed agendas it was an attempt to avoid the instrumental relationships that agendas typically precipitate. Instrumental relationships are subject-object relationships rather than person-to-person relationships. In Martin Buber's words, "I-It" rather than an "I-Thou." [3]

That said, it is clear that hierarchical structures in organizations are designed as a way to get work done through others. A manager's job, by definition, is instrumental and his or her relationship to subordinates is instrumental. If instrumental relationships are embedded in the way organizations are structured, is it not asking the impossible to encourage the holders of those positions to dialogue in a person-to-person relationship?

Perhaps what is necessary in organizations is to create opportunities to have frequent dialogue and through that dialogue to come to shared meaning. Then, with that co-created meaning as a foundation, individuals and groups could interact in more purposeful ways to make decisions and problem solve. I do not want to go so far as to say they would "engage in their normal way of interacting in business" because even when people interact in more purposeful ways than dialogue would support, it would be inconsistent to use others as instruments to accomplish a purpose without their full knowledge and uncoerced agreement with the purpose. In many organizations that caveat may not represent business as usual.

If there were frequent dialogue in our organizations, then the nature of people's relationships with each other might change. As Bohm said, "When you listen to somebody else, whether you like it or not, what they say becomes part of you."[4] Through dialogue it might be possible to alter taken-for-granted assumptions not only about what people are trying to accomplish together but also about how people structure their relationships. Putting collective intelligence to use, they might find some resolution to the management emphasis on instrumentality.

DIALOGUE AFFIRMS THE INTELLECTUAL CAPABILITY OF ORDINARY HUMAN BEINGS

Dialogue is based on the principle that the human mind is capable of using logic and reason to understand the world, rather than having to rely on the interpretation of someone who claims authority through force, tradition, superior intellect, or divine right. The theorists considered here are not the only ones who have faith in the ability of human beings to comprehend their world. Such faith is at the heart of Reginald Revans' Action Learning process[5] (see Chapter 6, below). It is also in the Theory Y that Douglas McGregor[6] suggested as an alternative to Theory X. More recently it is in the ideology that underlies Marvin Weisbord's advocacy of future search conferences[7] as well as Merrelyn Emery's[8] similar "whole system in a room" processes[8] (see also Chapter 6, below). And, of course, it underlies participative democracy.

Dialogue is an affirmation of the intellectual capability of not only the individual but also the collective. It acknowledges that everyone is blind to his or her own tacit assumptions and needs the help of others to see them. It acknowledges that each person, no matter how smart or capable, sees the world from a perspective and that there are other legitimate perspectives that could inform that view. People know this intellectually and yet have great difficulty living its reality. I am often struck by the language I hear when managers talk about such concepts as empowerment, participation, or even dialogue: "We want others to feel involved"; not "We need the ideas of others". "People will be more willing to change if they have had input into the change"; not "We need the ideas of others to understand how to make the change". The emphasis in managers' language is more often on the manipulation of the perception of others than on the need for or use of their collective intellect. Perhaps this language reflects ambivalence or perhaps it reflects a partial step toward the use of the collective intelligence.

THE OUTCOME OF DIALOGUE IS UNPREDICTABLE

It is not possible to anticipate the outcome of dialogue; if it were, there would be no need to engage in it. Because meaning is co-created in the act of dialogue, it cannot be known ahead of time what meaning will emerge. It is possible that some taken-for-granted assumptions may be raised that management would prefer be left alone, such as the differential in salary between upper management and workers, the organization's effect on the environment, or the overall purpose of the organization.

It would, however, be inconsistent to say to a group in dialogue: "Examine the paradigms under which you function so that those that are limiting can be altered, but do not examine anything that touches on issues of power or control." If a forum is created in which dialogue can occur, it must be accepted that some of the beliefs that people hold sacred will be challenged.

The unpredictability of dialogue may be problematic in yet another sense. That is, when resources are allocated for an organizational effort such as dialogue, people typically want some assurance up front about what outcomes might be expected. To do less would not be seen as exercising fiscal responsibility. Yet no one can anticipate where dialogue might go.

DIALOGUE IS PARADOXICAL

The practice of dialogue depends upon the organization having a climate that is open and respectful of individuals and where information is shared, members are free from coercion, and everyone has equal opportunity to challenge the ideas of others. Without such a climate, it is unlikely that either individuals or groups would expend the energy or incur the risks that would be needed for dialogue to take place. For example, it is unlikely that individuals would hold their opinions up for scrutiny in a climate where mistakes are seen as failure and the norm is to cover up what went wrong. It is equally unlikely that organizational members would challenge others if that challenge might be viewed as insubordination.

Thus a paradox exists. In order for organizational members to risk engaging in dialogue, the organization must have a climate that supports the development of individuals as well as the development of the organization. Yet that climate is unlikely to come into being until individuals are able to engage in dialogue. The individual and the norms of the system are so intertwined that attempts to change either without changing the other are not likely to succeed. To the extent that either individual actions or system norms are tacit the change becomes even more difficult.

That said, the only place such a change can begin is with individuals - not the individual in isolation but individuals in community. When a group of individuals begins to change, even a non-sanctioned group, the organization has begun to change. Perhaps the first step in moving beyond the paradox is to name it - that is, publicly to identify the situation in which organizations find themselves, to raise it to the level of public discussion, of dialogue.

SOURCES FOR CHAPTER 4

[1] Brookfield S D (1988) *Developing Critical Thinkers* Jossey-Bass, San Francisco.

[2] Freire P (1994) *Pedagogy of the Oppressed* Continuum Publishing, New York.

[3] Buber M (1970) *I and Thou* Charles Scribner's Sons, New York.

[4] Bohm D (1992) 'Dialogue as a Path Toward Wholeness' in Weisbord M (ed) *Discovering Common Ground* Berrett-Koehler, San Francisco. P.119.

[5] Revans R W (1980) *Action Learning: new techniques for management* Blond & Briggs, London; Revans R W (1998) *ABC of Action Learning* Lemos & Crane, London.

[6] McGregor D (1969) *The Human Side of Enterprise* McGraw-Hill, New York.

[7] Weisbord M (1992) *Discovering Common Ground* Berrett-Koehler, San Francisco.

[8] Emery M (ed) (1989) *Participative Design for Participative Democracy* Australian National University, Canberra.

5. How Dialogue can be incorporated into Work Processes

IN THIS CHAPTER: Examples of new work processes that organizations are exploring, or inventing, that include significant opportunities for dialogue.

Contents

CONDITIONS FOR VARIABLE DIALOGUE   *p. 74*

THE FORUM AS A "CONTAINER"   *p. 77*

DIALOGUE AS AN AGENT OF DEVELOPMENT   *p. 78*

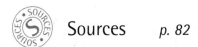 Sources   *p. 82*

5 How Dialogue Can Be Incorporated into Work Processes

It is doubtful that, in most organizations, dialogue could immediately be part of the regularly scheduled Monday morning staff meeting. The norms for how people relate to each other, what they can and cannot say, who they are supposed to be, may be too strong to overcome. The problem, of course, is that it is difficult to put aside the power and mistrust that keeps people from engaging in dialogue in the first place. If everything but the talk stays the same - that is, who makes the decisions, who sets the limits, who has special access to knowledge - then how can people relate in a different way? It is, I think, too much to expect people to position dialogue on top of the existing structure and have it be unfeigned.

I am also sceptical that dialogue can be promoted in the confines of a classroom or a retreat setting with any hope it will carry over to everyday work. Being in dialogue in the isolation of the classroom does not address or redress the many political and cultural issues that prevent people from being in dialogue in the work site. Moreover, I am convinced that people do not need to "learn" to speak their own truth, which they already know how.

There appears, however, to be an emerging alternative. There are a number of new work processes that organizations are exploring, or inventing, that incorporate significant opportunities for dialogue - often in large-group settings. These include strategic search conferences, open space technology, real-time strategic change, and action learning, to name a few of the most prominent. I want to refer to these collectively as "forums". In each of these forums a kind of container or holding environment is created in which dialogue about critical organizational issues occurs over a period of several days. The purpose of these forums is not to engage in dialogue. Rather dialogue is the vehicle through which work is examined and accomplished within the forum. That difference would appear to be an important one for organizational settings that dialogue is a way of getting work done, not an end in itself.

Although critical work is accomplished, these forums are far from being "business as usual". The container or holding environment that is created incorporates many of the elements of dialogue that are proposed by the five theorists discussed in this paper. Thus, the forums embody fundamentally different conditions from those in which people usually talk with each other. It is also important to note that the forums address a specific issue that is critical to the organization such as a problem that needs solving or a strategy that needs to be developed. They are not exercises or hypothetical situations but the real work of the organization. The dialogue that ensues is about issues that participants care about and in which they have considerable stake.

CONDITIONS FOR VIABLE DIALOGUE

My intent here is not to advocate these particular forums but to use them to illustrate how organizations may be incorporating dialogue in a more acceptable way. (I have placed a brief description of each of the forums in Chapter 6, below.) Although these forums vary greatly in terms of such elements as method and size, they share a number of conditions that make dialogue viable.

Empowerment of the group

First, top management agrees, well before the event, to relinquish power to the forum to make changes. This is very different from the more familiar situation in which a group makes recommendations to the management who may decide, at a later date, whether or not to implement them. What legitimizes this empowerment of the group is that all of the knowledge that exists in the organization about the issue being addressed is invited into the room. Furthermore, all of the knowledge that is in the room is available to everyone. When everyone comes to know what everyone else knows about the issue, a delay to seek a wider or more informed view is no longer valid. A forum in which such an up-front agreement has been made represents a fundamental change in the distribution of power and control in the organization, albeit a temporary one.

Equality among participants

Second, in these forums measures are taken to reduce the effects of hierarchy because such effects have an acknowledged tendency to limit dialogue. Most of the forums are facilitated not by management but by a "third party". Often management does not play a central or visible role. There are no introductory speeches about the need to change or the importance of the task, and no closing remarks are made in appreciation of the effort of the troops. In some of these forums, management is not in the room at all. In others, management is present but has been coached to be parsimonious with its contributions. There is a strong component of self-management in the forums; process issues that arise are resolved in the small groups or in the total group. There are basic guidelines embodied in the structure of the forum (these vary with different types of forums) which are typically established at the beginning by consent of the whole, but these are often minimal and alterable. The diminished role of management and the focus on self-management significantly reduce the influence of status and rank and create an equality among participants that facilitates the dialogue.

Collective intelligence

Third, the assumption is made that the group that has come together is capable of both understanding and resolving the issue with which they are faced. There are no experts or consultants present to advise how the issue should be addressed. The necessary information and expertise, which are typically diverse, are embedded in the people in the room, who come from different parts of the organization and from multiple levels. Often customers and suppliers are invited, adding yet more diversity of perspective. It is the collective intelligence of the group, expressed through dialogue, which is sought as the source of new understanding. In referencing search conferences specifically, Weisbord said, "We believe the real world is knowable to ordinary people and their knowledge can be collectively and meaningfully organized. In fact, ordinary people are an extraordinary source of information about the real world."[1]

This willingness to trust in collective intelligence rather than "expert" opinion requires a major shift in thinking about where the "true" source of knowledge resides in organizations. In most organizations people are more comfortable with having experts construct an answer, although the need for everyone to discuss it and eventually "buy in" is acknowledged.

Mixed interactions

Fourth, these forums are often a mixture of small- and large-group interactions. The small groups provide the opportunity to participate that often does not exist in large groups. Yet the large group is critical to contain the sense of the whole. The alternation between small groups and the large group encourages individuals and functional groups to challenge, question, refute, and reflect and to hear others do the same. Yet the context is co-operative. There is an agreed-upon goal toward which the total group is striving and which the controversy serves. Forums occur over an extended period of time, often several days, allowing individuals to build the trust and respect for each other that can accommodate challenge. This mixture of challenge and co-operation may also represent a major shift in thinking from organizational norms in which questioning is considered resistance to change and challenge is acceptable only when it is directed downward.

THE FORUM AS A "CONTAINER"

I have called these forums a container and I think the figure is useful. It is as if people can experiment within this contained space. It is a place to try out things that are too risky to permit in day-to-day work. There is safety in the confines of the container where people agree to function differently but also agree to the time and space limits. Organizations may initially need these "contained" times and spaces where organizational members can experience what it is like to be in a different type of relationship with each other. Then, over time, perhaps the new way of talking, the new way of being with each other can encroach into the day-to-day activities of the organization, so that the staff meeting or the planning meeting becomes more dialogic. If people can act in these "contained" spaces in ways that are more open and egalitarian, and if they can share power more fully, then, over time, the power and structure of the organization may shift and the organization may, in fact, develop.

DIALOGUE AS AN AGENT OF DEVELOPMENT

These forums and techniques can lead to development of an organization by two means: first, by virtue of the content of the dialogue itself, and, second, by the nature of the interaction, which has the potential to alter the political and relationship structure of the organization.

With respect to the first means, the forums discussed here address a specific organizational issue. Through the dialogue that occurs, the collective intelligence of the organization is brought to bear on that issue. As Johnson and Johnson noted, the result is likely to be an understanding of the issue that is richer, more integrated, and more creative than any one individual or homogeneous group is likely to produce. This new understanding may lead to more productive actions and decisions. Additionally, each individual engaged in the dialogue is likely to come away with greater comprehension of the issue and thus a commitment to subsequent actions. I am proposing an outcome that is more complex than the truism that people will support what they have some say in. I suggest that it is not involvement that commits organizational members. Rather it is: (1) the engagement of their reasoning; (2) their mental wrestling with the complexity of the issue; and (3) the fuller understanding those mental processes produce that make the position arrived at more acceptable, regardless of whether it corresponds with one's own. The organization develops through the new understandings that are borne of the dialogue.

With respect to the second means, dialogue changes the nature of the interaction. Through dialogue, individuals experience themselves in different political relationships with each other. Engaging in a forum in which power has been transferred to the collective can lay the foundation for the group to question the status quo in which the collective is not so empowered. Organizational members might reason: "Clearly this group, as a whole, understands this issue better than any single individual or single group, regardless of their position in the organization. Why are we empowered around this issue and not others that are equally critical to us? Perhaps addressing critical issues collectively should be the norm."

Likewise, interacting as equals may lead organizational members to recognize that they are, in fact, equal in intellectual capability, reasoning, and knowledge and therefore that others have less right to special privileges or deference. They may come to question the basis that legitimizes others giving direction, receiving disproportional compensation, or withholding information.

Finally, self-managing the process of the forum may convince organizational members that they are capable of self-management in general and do not need experts or management to shepherd them through processes. They may come to believe in their own collective capability to design actions that lead to greater productivity and development.

★

The historical development of organizations has been in the direction of greater flexibility, adaptability, and ability to take into account a more comprehensive, and recently, a more global perspective. This development has come about through a consistent shift away from autocracy and bureaucracy and toward increased participation - a shift in the locus of power. As Peter Block said,

> *"Often our focus on change is aimed at better*
> *communication, working as a team, meeting to decide*
> *how to cut costs, and giving recognition for exceptional*
> *contributions. These actions do not change the rules,*
> *they simply help us better adapt to the same game.*
> *For the game to change, hard currency has to change*
> *hands. In organizations, hard currency is rearranging*
> *who makes choices, who defines culture, who*
> *determines the measures, and who shares in the*
> *wealth."* [2]

The forums discussed here allow organizational members to experience themselves in a different relationship with each other and with the whole of the organization. This opens the door to altering the fundamental power and structure in the organization.

Conclusion

I find the emergence of such forums a promising sign that our organizations are capable of becoming more dialogic. I am also encouraged that there seem to be a growing number of such forums in a variety of shapes and formats. However, I do not want to suggest that these forums are the only ways in which dialogue can emerge within organizations. There have certainly been other examples of organizational practices that point in the same direction - for instance, group meetings in which a "devil's advocate" is regularly appointed or project teams which purposively include a naive member to ask the taken-for-granted questions. These techniques are far from being dialogue as it is described here, yet they show a direction, a growing intent in organizations to institutionalize dialogue.

Dialogue offers organizations the possibility of developing individuals and systems that are better able to handle the complexity of this diverse and fast-changing world. But it is a non-scientific solution in an age in which people are most comfortable trusting science. It is a long-term solution at a time when people want immediate answers.

Yet it is consonant with other changes in organizations, such as empowerment, self-managed teams, and reduction in layers of management. This is an interesting age. It has one foot in the traditions of the past and one foot testing the ground of new ways to function. Dialogue is a tool of the new ground. It may also be a tool to help discover where the new ground lies.

Sources For Chapter 5

[1] Weisbord M (1992) *Discovering Common Ground* Berrett-Koehler, San Francisco, p.13.
[2] Block P (1993) *Stewardship* Berrett-Koehler, San Francisco, p.53.

6. Forums and Conditions for Dialogue

IN THIS CHAPTER: The first part of this chapter considers the group settings that provide opportunities for dialogue, which I collectively call "forums". The second part sets out the practical "speech acts" and "situation variables" involved in dialogue.

Contents

FORUMS FOR DIALOGUE   *p. 85*

    Future Search Conferences   *p. 85*

    Open Space Technology   *p. 86*

    Action Learning   *p. 88*

    Real-time Strategic Change   *p. 90*

    Team Syntegrity   *p. 91*

THE CONDITIONS FOR DIALOGUE   *p. 92*

    Speech acts   *p. 93*

    Situation variables   *p. 94*

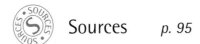 Sources   *p. 95*

6 Forums and Conditions for Dialogue

FORUMS FOR DIALOGUE

Collectively I refer to the group settings that provide opportunities for dialogue as 'forums'. The examples I discuss here are future search conferences, open space technology, action learning, real-time strategic change and team syntegrity.

Future Search Conferences

Marvin Weisbord has popularized a process, which he calls the "future search conference",[1] for involving the whole organization in the development of strategy. A typical search conference brings together 30 to 80 people for 16 hours across three days. Together they engage in a series of tasks that involve exploring the organization's past, present, and preferred future. The process is basically a democratic one, reminiscent of town meetings. There are neither lectures by experts nor vision statements by leadership. The purpose is to learn together about a preferred future and to make that future happen. Each part of the conference - past, present, and future - has four elements:

- to build a database,
- to look at it together,

- to interpret what is found, and
- to draw conclusions for action.

The three days of the future search conference are preceded by a lengthy period of planning. A small group, representative of the prospective participants, meets with the conference facilitators to select the attendees and to communicate the search purpose and plan. A conference typically involves a wide diversity of participants, including customers and suppliers. The conference itself is facilitated by a team trained in the conference model.

The work of the search conference alternates between the large group and teams of approximately eight. Homogeneous, functional teams accomplish some of the tasks, whereas other tasks are accomplished in mixed stakeholder teams. The teams self-manage their semi-structured dialogue. The intent of the dialogue is not to resolve conflicts but to find "common ground all can stand on without forcing or compromising." The search conference seeks "to hear and appreciate differences, not reconcile them." [2]

There are conclusions drawn at three levels: those for *individual use*, which each individual keeps; those for the *functional level*, which are reviewed at the meeting by the department personnel; and those that go *across functions*, which are reviewed at the conference by the top-management group. At each level, action plans are drawn up and agreed to, based on the conclusions.

Open Space Technology

Open space technology is a meeting format developed by Harrison Owen. Its purpose is to create a space in which breakthrough ideas can emerge. An open space conference is held in a large room without much furniture but with a great deal of wall space to post ideas and notices. A typical conference lasts for two to three days. The essence of the conference is embedded in the rules Owen[3] has constructed for it:

- There is no agenda, but there is a theme that is stated at the beginning of the conference.
- No one is in charge.
- The meeting starts with everyone standing or sitting in a circle where they can see each other.
- Each participant who chooses identifies an issue related to the theme for which he or she is willing to take responsibility for holding a discussion. The topic is announced and then posted so that others can join. The identification of topics continues until all ideas have been exhausted.
- When all the ideas are out, participants sign up for the groups that are of particular interest to them.
- The sponsor of each group convenes the group at the appointed time, leads the discussion, and takes notes.
- The notes from all of the meetings are typed into a bank of computers and made immediately available to everyone.
- Each day of the conference, the topic identification and subsequent discussions are continued.
- "The rule of two feet" says that if a participant is bored or has nothing to contribute to a group, he or she should "honour the group" and leave to join a group that is of more interest.

According to Owen, the lack of form allows ideas to take their own shape, undistorted by status or politics. The facilitation for open space involves little more than establishing the purpose initially and outlining the minimal open-space guidelines as listed above.

Action Learning

Action Learning is a process developed by Reginald Revans over fifty years ago in the coalfields of England. He involved managers in the resolution of their own production problems, an unheard of idea in 1945.

Purpose and process

Action Learning has two goals:

- to benefit the organization by addressing perplexing problems that have heretofore been insoluble, and
- to benefit individuals by making it possible for them to learn with and from others by discussing the difficulties each member of the action set experiences while working on a significant organizational problem.

A typical Action Learning programme begins with a large-group workshop of three to five days in length. Following the workshop, small groups are formed to address specific organizational problems. The groups meet with or without a facilitator on a weekly or bi-weekly basis over a lengthy period, perhaps six to nine months. The groups meet for a full or half-day depending upon the nature of the problem and the constraints of the organization. Halfway through this time all the groups may come together again for three to five days to exchange information. A final meeting of three to five days is usually planned at the end.

The nature of the problems that the groups address is critical. First, they are problems that are important to the organization, not made-up exercises. Second, the problems are complex in nature, dealing with systemic organizational issues. Third, they are problems that are not amenable to expert solutions nor have ready-made right answers.

Action Learning differs from more typical cross-functional task forces in that Action Learning groups are charged with learning from the problems they are solving; that means assumptions are challenged and actions are confronted. In conventional task teams the major goal is to address the problem; any learning that occurs is incidental. A second difference is that Action Learning groups are charged with implementation as well as planning. Much of the learning from an Action Learning problem comes from attempting to garner the support and face the problems inherent in implementation. A third difference is that Action Learning groups address unfamiliar problems rather than problems in which they already have expertise, as might be more common in task forces or process-improvement teams. Addressing unfamiliar problems results in fresh perspectives being brought to bear on problems and provides individuals the opportunity to learn new ways to address problems.

Underlying principles

Action Learning is based on adult learning principles, which hold that:

- managers learn best from each other
- managers learn from reflecting on how they are addressing real problems
- managers learn when they are able to question the assumptions on which their actions are based, and
- managers learn when they receive accurate feedback from others and from the results of their problem-solving actions.

Likewise, Action Learning is based on organizational principles that hold that:

- organizational issues are solvable by organizational members who care about the issues; and
- organizational members who have not previously been involved in the issue can offer a fresh perspective that results in innovative solutions.

There are numerous variations of Action Learning which have been successfully implemented in different organizations. Action Learning can vary in terms of the composition of the groups, that is, across organizations, functions, and departments. It can also vary in terms of the length of time and frequency with which groups meet.

Real-time Strategic Change

The use of the term "real time" refers to the simultaneous planning and implementation of change. This whole-system-in-the-room process addresses the current issues of the organization in terms of their interconnections with the entire organizational system. All or a critical mass of the people in an organization from all levels are involved, including key internal and external stakeholders. This widespread involvement serves three purposes:

1 A data-rich, complex, clear, composite picture of the organization's reality can be constructed by integrating the many perspectives represented.
2 Shared insights that emerge from this more informed view pave the way for establishing internal and external partnerships that previously would have made no sense when stakeholders operated solely out of their limited perspectives.
3 All essential stakeholders understand, accept, and

can start to use these broad, whole-picture views in deciding how they want and need to do business in the future.[4]

Real-time strategic change involves up to 2,000 people in three-day meetings. The three days are based on having a flow of information from the individual, to the small group, to the whole group, and back again. To accomplish this, conference facilitators set task and time limits. However, the discussions that go on within the groups are not structured. The intent is to control the process, not the content. There is an emphasis on truth telling and honesty.

Real-time strategic change involves a more active role of the organization's leadership than do some of the other forums described here. For example, the meeting begins with a welcome from the organization leadership to highlight the importance of the event and the power of the group to shape the organization's strategy. Times are set aside for the leadership to respond to questions formulated by mixed-table discussions; and the leadership is tasked with constructing a strategy based on the data generated by the mixed groups.

Team Syntegrity

Team Syntegrity, originated by Stafford Beer (1994), is based on the polyhedral geometry of Buckminster Fuller. The process brings together thirty participants from different parts of the organization around a topic that requires breakthrough thinking. The thirty identify twelve themes important to the topic. The group holds a sequence of meetings based on the "nodes" of the polyhedron, so that by the end of the three or five day period 36 meetings (the 36 sides of the polyhedron) have been held to explore the twelve topics. The quintessential feature is that eleven of the twelve are represented in every meeting so that not only are diverse perspectives brought to bear on the topics but also the relationship of the topics to each other is thoroughly examined. The configuration of the repeated discussions create a synergy around key ideas and work to prevent the ideas of high status persons from dominating. The result is innovative ideas that grow out of the collective interpretation as well as a commitment to move forward in the directions the group has developed. Follow up meetings in the work site again make use of the polyhedral configuration to maintain the momentum and alignment that were initiated at the first meeting.

THE CONDITIONS FOR DIALOGUE

In the second part of this chapter I have placed the major constructs of the theorists discussed in Chapter 3 into two categories. The first is "speech acts", by which I mean what individuals who are engaging in dialogue actually do; and the second is "situation variables", which are the norms and conditions under which the speech acts are exercised. In developing the consolidated summary list shown below, I have stated each construct in the language of one specific theorist and then attached to it the names of theorists who are in agreement with that construct. In some cases, this may do disservice to the theorist whose language is not represented. Moreover, the first list is more heavily weighted with the ideas of Argyris and of Johnson and Johnson, who focused more on technique than Freire, Bohm, and Mezirow.

Speech acts in dialogue

Provide others with accurate and complete information including feelings that bear upon the issue. (*Argyris; Johnson and Johnson; Mezirow*)

Advocate one's own position. (*Argyris; Johnson and Johnson*)

Make the reasoning in one's own views explicit - say how one got from the data to one's conclusion. (*Argyris*)

Invite others to comment on or inquire into one's own reasoning. (*Argyris; Bohm*)

Identify reasoning errors in others. (*Argyris; Johnson and Johnson*)

When others' view differs from one's own, inquire into others' reasoning. (*Argyris; Bohm*)

Confirm others' personal competence when disagreeing with their ideas. (*Johnson and Johnson*)

Design ways to test competing views. (*Argyris*)

Regard assertions (one's own and others') as hypotheses-to-be-tested. (*Argyris; Bohm*)

Voice the perspective of others (*Johnson and Johnson; Mezirow; Argyris.*)

Change position when others offer convincing data and rationale. (*Argyris; Johnson and Johnson*)

Illustrate and publicly test inferences. (*Argyris*)

Back up generalizations with concrete examples. (*Johnson and Johnson; Argyris*)

Advocate the exertion of effort to achieve mutual goals. (*Johnson and Johnson*)

Acknowledge similarities in ideas as well as differences. (*Johnson and Johnson*)

Reflect critically upon presuppositions and their consequences. (*Mezirow; Argyris; Bohm; Freire*)

Weigh evidence and assess arguments objectively. (*Mezirow*)

Situation variables in dialogue

Members feel free from coercion. (*Mezirow; Johnson and Johnson; Argyris; Bohm; Freire*)

Participants have equal opportunity to participate - including the chance to challenge, question, refute, and reflect and to hear others do the same. (*Argyris; Johnson and Johnson; Bohm; Mezirow*)

Participants are heterogeneous in terms of such factors as personality, sex, attitudes, diverse experiences, and ability levels. (*Johnson and Johnson*)

The context is co-operative, individuals feel it is safe to challenge each other, and controversy is viewed as constructive. (*Johnson and Johnson; Argyris*)

Information and expertise are distributed among participants, and participants do not feel the need to defer to one individual. (*Johnson and Johnson; Freire*)

Meetings are held without purpose or agenda.(*Bohm*)

Groups have positive outcome interdependence. (*Johnson and Johnson*)

Groups have means interdependence. (*Johnson and Johnson*)

Sources for Chapter 6

[1] Weisbord M (1992) *Discovering Common Ground* Berrett-Koehler, San Francisco.
[2] Weisbord M (1992) *ibid*, p.7.
[3] Owen H (1992) *Riding the Tiger: doing business in a transforming world* Abbott Publishing, Potomac MD.
[4] Jacobs R W (1994) *Real Time Strategic Change* Berrett-Koehler, San Francisco.

7. Dialogue Practices in Organizations

IN THIS CHAPTER: The ways dialogue is being used in organizations, as well as methods to introduce and improve dialogue.

Contents

STRUCTURING THE DIALOGUE   *p. 100*

CREATING THE DIALOGUE   *p. 105*

TIMING THE DIALOGUE   *p. 115*

THE QUESTION OF FACILITATION   *p. 118*

IMPROVING THE DIALOGUE   *p. 123*

THE PARADOX OF DIALOGUE   *p. 127*

 Sources   *p. 129*

7 Dialogue Practices in Organizations

There are many places where dialogue is critical: family, church, public interest groups, and work. Of these, work is the most problematic because of our strong organizational norms against talk that is not instrumental. Bird and Waters identified an interesting phenomena which they labeled, "the moral muteness of managers." [1] They suggest that managers often recognize that they are facing a moral issue in their work and they privately invoke moral standards to deal with the issue. However, they are reluctant to acknowledge those standards in workplace discussions. Rather they couch their reasoning in rational terms. In fact, from interviews with 60 managers, Bird and Waters found nearly 300 cases in which the managers had faced moral issues in their work, but in only 12 per cent of these cases was there any public discussion of the moral issues.

Organizational members need a place to raise and address the issues that matter to them, whether those are moral issues, hopes for the future, or new ways to function. We come to work as full human beings with our values, morals, skills, knowledge, and hopes intact. If we are to grow and develop as human beings we must have the opportunity to bring all of ourselves to work. Current norms, notwithstanding, organizational members are finding ways to hold such dialogues. In this chapter, I have suggested some ways dialogue is being used in organizations, as well as some ways to introduce and improve dialogue.

STRUCTURING THE DIALOGUE

Our surroundings have a powerful impact on how we interact with each other. Yet, often we give this important element too little consideration. The space we talk within, the size of the group, the formality of the setting, often seem more like a convenience (or inconvenience) to which we have to adapt or "make the best of", rather than something to be purposeful about.

Nonetheless, our surroundings provide us with strong cues to which we respond, often without even recognizing them as such. From such cues we determine:

- who is important - office size and accoutrements tell us much about a person's position.
- how formal or informal the conversation is supposed to be - whether someone sits behind a desk or joins you at a table says much about the conversation you can expect to have.
- the nature of the relationship - you probably wouldn't offer a cup of coffee to someone you were getting ready to reprimand.

The environment in which we talk with others often says as much as the words we choose. Researchers have only begun to consider the ways in which the space we occupy helps or hinders the way we talk with each other. In the next section, we look at some of the issues of structure and size that affect the nature of the dialogue.

A circle makes the difference – a big difference

The arrangement in which people sit has the most important consequences for dialogue. A circle is the only configuration that manifests equal participation – which is so central to dialogue. In a circle there is no "head of the table," no place where all eyes are naturally focused like the front of the room or the open end of a "U." A circle allows everyone to see the eyes of everyone else. However, the shape of a room can make it difficult to form a true circle. If some people are slightly pushed back from the circle so that they cannot make eye contact with those on either side without turning their heads, you may need to ask the members of the group to adjust their chairs until everyone has a clear line of vision with everyone else. A circle does not have desks or tables in front of people. There is a very different feel to a circle when tables are in front of the participants. It feels less open and less intense.

Participants often initially resist moving into a circle. They voice any number of reasons for not wanting to create a circle; "Why do we have to go to the trouble of moving?" "We won't have anything to write on." "I need a table to put my things on." There is no question that a circle engenders feelings of vulnerability, of being "out there" that, particularly in a new group, are a little uncomfortable. However, the feelings of discomfort are usually short lived. Within a few minutes, participants are leaning forward in their chairs, fully engaged in the dialogue and any initial misgivings about the seating arrangement have been set aside.

It is helpful, if each time the group meets, members sit in a different location in the circle. We all have an inclination to return to a seat or place we have already made familiar – we may even feel that we are usurping someone else's chair if we move. However, that very familiarity has the downside of "cueing" participants to remember past reactions, ideas, and feelings. A new seating arrangement provides a fresh start. It allows each person to put aside the assumptions and feelings about others that they may have held over, even tacitly, from the last meeting. In addition, by virtue of the forward placement of the eyes in the human face, we tend to have greater eye contact with those who are across from us and less with those who are beside us. Changing where we sit allows us to connect with those that we may have previously had less connection with and to re-connect in a new way.

With a group that meets for many different reasons (e.g. staff meeting, to hear a lecture, to problem solve), moving into a circle differentiates the time when participants are in dialogue from the times when they are in other types of meetings. So the circle becomes an important physical reminder of that difference. Without such a visible reminder it might be too easy to slip into problem solving or speech making.

Size of the group for speaking and reflecting

Bohm suggests that an ideal number for a dialogue is 40, a number, he says, that is large enough to have within it all aspects of a mini-society. However, many people, myself included, find 20 a more functional number for dialogue. With 20 people there is still diversity of opinion so necessary to dialogue and the smaller number allows more "air time" for each participant.

However, even with 20, there are people who will say very little during the dialogue. That need not be an overriding consideration, after all, dialogue is not only about talking, it is equally about reflecting. I don't need "air time" in order to notice my reaction to what is being said, to suspend my judgement intentionally, or to listen "generatively" (i.e. with the intention of learning from the other). I can learn a great deal about myself and how I think by attending to what is going on with my internal talk and by being aware of the physical cues my body is giving me through my posture and level of alertness. If I exercise some restraint, someone else may give voice to the idea I would have raised, so I do not need to raise it myself. Although another may voice my thought, I am the only one who can notice my own assumptions and reflect on the meaning of what I am hearing. Reflection is a critical part of dialogue and, fortunately, it is not affected by the size of the group.

Making a space for dialogue

Some organizations have created special places designed to be more conducive to dialogue than the traditional conference room. These are less formal spaces, often with comfortable couches and overstuffed chairs. They have more natural lighting than the harsh florescent lights of conference rooms and they typically have coffee and refreshments handy. There are a few examples here that illustrate how organizations are thinking about space for dialogue.

Steelcase Corporation, itself an office furniture manufacturer, has created office areas that are designed as "neighbourhoods". Product and business teams that work together are located near each other in the neighbourhood and there is a community "commons', where informal conversation and community interaction occur. Studies have shown that the availability of the "commons" actually serves to increase collaboration among team members. [2] The idea of pulsing between a "personal harbour" where team members can focus on individual work and a "commons" area designed for collaboration, is for many, the office design of the future.

Many other companies (for example, Hitachi America Ltd, National City Bank, Owens Corning) have developed similar shared space, often with the design help of Steelcase. SAS Airlines in Stockholm has a "central plaza" in the midst of its corporate headquarters. The plaza contains shops and a café where people from all levels and functions are encouraged to visit and share ideas. These designs reflect the increasingly relational nature of our work and the importance of creating space that accommodates a more relational kind of talk.

Haworth, another office furniture company, has a room it calls the "Mind Field". This is a room set aside for the meetings of the "ideation team" at Haworth. It is a large but very informal room, with couches and comfortable chairs arranged in a conversational grouping. The walls of the room are covered with whiteboards and additional whiteboards are scattered throughout the room. The whiteboards are filled with diagrams, lists, pictures, quotes, charts and other thinking tools the team has used. In addition, flowing through these many items are arrows connecting ideas to each other. The way the team works in this room is that when the group comes up with an idea they think is important, someone writes it up on the whiteboard. It is possible to see (literally) how that idea connects to other ideas the team has had because the team has instituted a "no erase" policy. Sometimes team members rearrange the ideas on the boards or subsume one under another, but the intent is to keep these important ideas in front of them as they work to assist members to build the connections that inform their thinking. This room is a physical representation of the idea that rather than dismissing conflicting ideas quickly, in dialogue, we need to hold on to dissonance long enough to see behind it to the connections and assumptions that underlie it.

The managers of a Siemens factory in North Carolina were uncomfortable with the amount of time that workers spent chatting in the cafeteria. There was talk about how to curb such an unproductive use of time until a group of researchers from the Center for Workforce Development provided data about what was really happening in the cafeteria. The study showed that during a typical week, more than 70 per cent of the 1,000 workers who participated in the study said they shared information with co-workers while in the cafeteria, while 55 per cent said they asked co-workers for advice while there. The study convinced Siemens' management that they ought to be facilitating these conversations rather than hindering them. As a result they placed empty pads of paper and overhead projectors in the lunchroom to facilitate informal meetings. The findings from this intriguing study remind us that people want and need to talk about the issues that are central to their work and that the formal meetings we hold in organizations are not often conducive to that kind of talk.

CREATING THE DIALOGUE

One of the things that makes dialogue problematic in organizations is the limits we put on what we can talk about. Many of these limitations spring from real concerns about getting into trouble for raising an issue. Some of the limitations come from a feeling that certain issues are just inappropriate for an organizational setting, and some limitations are there because the subject has become so familiar that we have lost awareness of it. In this section, we explore the limitations on what we talk about in more depth.

We already know how to talk

I assert in this book that "we already know how to talk," that we already have the skills necessary to hold an in-depth, relational, assumption suspending dialogue (see Chapter 4). One of the ways you can assure yourself or the group about this point is to ask each member of the group to:

- Tell about a person with whom you have the best conversations. It can be some one from your past, your family, work, or whatever.
- What are the qualities of the situation that makes these conversations exemplary?

When I do this exercise with groups, I allow a lot of time because the people that participants talk about are very important to them and they enjoy remembering these conversations - they are often reluctant to yield the floor. You can see how positive they feel about these situations by the way they smile or "light up" as they talk. Their posture becomes more relaxed and open, their talk often slows, and their voices take on a thoughtful tone.

When we have gone around the circle, I ask the group to think with me about the patterns they heard in the stories. Invariably the patterns that we note are about the nature of the relationship, not the skill of the other, or even the storyteller's own skill. After such an exercise I am often again reminded that our too frequently poor conversations in organizations are not because we lack skill, but because we are so fearful (or political) about what and how we talk.

Raising "undiscussables"

In every organization there are topics that everyone knows about but which are not talked about openly and thus are not dealt with. These are sometimes called "undiscussables". In part, what keeps such topics out of an organizational dialogue is that participants are concerned that they may be the only person who is thinking a certain way. The following activity provides a safe way to raise some of the issues about which there is usually silence. Its design provides a measure of safety because participants can raise a topic anonymously. If they find that others are thinking in the same way, as often happens, then they may feel more willing to bring that idea up in a time of dialogue.

Activity

Stage 1   It is helpful to begin this exercise with assurance to the participants about who will have access to the items that they generate. It is probably most reasonable to gain agreement among members that the items and discussion will remain in the room. It may be that by the end of the exercise the group will alter that agreement, but that should only happen with full concurrence.

Stage 2   Each person is given five 3x5 inch "stickies" and asked to write at least one issue that they think is an "undiscussable". It is helpful to limit the range of items to those things that are undiscussable in this particular group - "What do *we* not discuss?" - because these are the only topics for which this group can take responsibility. Each person may write as many as five issues, one to a sticky. Give everyone a few minutes to think and write. Ask people to write a full sentence, not just a word or phrase like "money". Because the statements on the stickies are to remain anonymous, they need to be worded in a way that makes the idea very clear to a reader without further explanation. Sometimes an issue is so obvious to a participant that she or he thinks one word or short phrase says it all, for example, "corporate visits" but such a phrase for one participant may mean "we spend so much time getting ready for corporate visits we can't get our work done" and for another person may mean "certain groups are singled out during a corporate visit for much more attention than other groups" so fuller statements are essential. Participants' handwriting is often difficult to read so printing is better than cursive and big letters are more readable than small.

Stage 3   When participants have finished writing, ask everyone to place their stickies on the wall, randomly, so they cannot be identified by who wrote them. These need to be well distributed over a large wall.

Stage 4   Next the whole group spends some time reading the wall; getting very well acquainted with what is written there.

Stage 5   Then the group re-orders the stickies into categories (if the group is too large a facilitator can read each and place it in a category the group selects). This re-ordering can be somewhat chaotic but seems to work. Although some individuals always tend to take the lead in this part of the exercise, it is important to encourage everyone to engage in the re-ordering because participants begin the dialogue about the items as they re-order them. And it is the dialogue that starts to reduce the silence about the undiscussables.

Stage 6   Finally, as a group, the participants assign each category a name. This renaming may cause some items to be moved or a large grouping to be sub-divided. Again the names should not just be simple words such as "decision making" but full phrases that express the central idea within the items of the category, such as, "confusion about when the group versus the boss will make a decision".

Stage 7   Discussion follows next: A number of different discussions can occur based on the undiscussables and the categories of undiscussables the group has constructed. Since the purpose of this exercise is to get undiscussables on the table, it is critical to allow enough time for lengthy discussion or several lengthy discussions. These discussions can be held either in the full group (if it is not too large) or in sub-groups. Initially the discussions may be tentative or limited because of the concerns of members. That tentativeness usually disappears over time as participants come to see that others in the group have similar concerns and that there is no retribution for discussing these topics. The following topics related to the undiscussables may be useful:

- What makes this category so difficult to talk about?
- What problems does the silence about this topic exacerbate?
- How can we keep this category "on the table" for continued discussion after this series of meetings?

The paradox of this activity is, of course, that in identifying and categorizing the undiscussables, participants have begun, in fact, to discuss them.

Right and left-hand column

Those familiar with Argyris' work will recognize this as a variation on right/left hand column cases. This is a useful exercise to do with a team that works together on a regular basis. The purpose of the exercise is to see what inferences team members make about each other that are not openly tested. It is also a way to see if the team wants to invest time in learning the Model II skills that Argyris advocates. The activity might be spread over several days. At least two hours should be allotted for the last step.

Activity

Step 1   As a group, identify an event or incident that happened during a group meeting and that is regarded by members as puzzling. Choose one that was important enough that everyone remembers, but not one that is still acrimonious.

Step 2 Ask one member of the team to write out the conversation the group had as he/she remembers it. A page or two of conversation will suffice, it should not be the whole of a meeting or a lengthy conversation. It should, however, be written as a script rather than paraphrases of what people said.

Step 3 Pass the completed script around to one or two other members so that they can correct it or add to it from their memories. The goal is to get an approximation, not a completely accurate transcript.

Step 4 When the script has been generally agreed to, rewrite it so that the conversation is on the right hand side of the page and the left-hand side is left blank.

Step 5 Now ask each member of the team (including those who do not speak in the script, but were present at the meeting) to write into the left hand column what they were thinking or feeling but not saying in response to each part of the conversation on the right. Obviously, members will not be able to remember everything; a best approximation is perfectly adequate. Again, this column needs to be their thoughts, (e.g. "What does he mean by that?") not their paraphrase of their thoughts, (e.g. "I was confused at this point").

Step 6   Team members do not need to put their names on the completed scripts but copies of each script should be provided for all members; thus, everyone knows what is in everyone else's left-hand column.

Step 7   Together the group examines the scripts and looks for the inferences they make. They may note that different people construct conflicting inferences from the same part of the conversation. They may note patterns in the kind of inferences members make about each other.

Like the previous Activity, this process "puts on the table" things that team members may have been thinking but not saying, "undiscussables". The team, having discussed a topic in this way, may find it easier to address when it arises in other settings. As Argyris has frequently noted, not only are topics sometimes undiscussable, their undiscussability may also be undiscussable. This activity removes at least the first layer of secrecy. It can also serve as an introduction to Argyris' work and provide an opportunity for a team to determine if they want to invest in the lengthy process of developing the Model II skills that would allow them to test their inferences more publicly and that would assist them in using both advocacy and inquiry. These are difficult skills for a team to develop without initial assistance from someone who has expertise in the Model II skills, so it is a costly investment in both time and money. This Activity can provide an initial experience on which to make that judgment.

Dialoguing about what matters, and everything matters

Earlier in this book, I noted that much of the talk in organizations is instrumental in nature, that it is for the purpose of getting others "to agree" or "to do". If, however, dialogue is not instrumental, then what, in an organizational setting, do members have to say to each other? What is the topic of their proposed dialogue? I am often asked these questions. The questions themselves reveal the instrumental nature of our thinking about organizational conversation. What would we talk about if not about how to get something done?

For me, the answer lies in the differentiation between means and ends. Instrumental conversations are often about how – the "means" to get something accomplished. "Means" conversations are very necessary within our organizations and I want neither to end them nor limit them. However, they are not the only conversations we need to have. Organizational members also need to be engaged in dialogue about the "why" or the "ends" the organization serves; dialogue that continually examines the worth of the organization's purpose. Not as a one time event, but as an on-going dialogue. Moreover, as Freire would affirm, through such a dialogue organizational members "become co-participants in the creation, maintenance, and transformation" of the organizational reality.

In corporate settings members often leave the "ends" discussion to top management, seeing it as their prerogative. However, I want to advocate that any human system is in jeopardy when members view themselves as responsible only for the means, leaving it to others to determine the goal toward which the means are enacted.

Means and ends are inexorably linked and need to be continually re-examined and challenged. One of the dangers we are always susceptible to is allowing means to become ends. Organizational members cannot absolve themselves of the responsibility of insuring that the goal(s) toward which they are working is (are) worthy and that the means has not become confused with the ends.

I believe it is the responsibility of organizational members to be cognizant of the goal (the ends) which their work serves and when they see ways in which the goal is limited or questionable, it is their responsibility to engage in public dialogue to challenge or question it. By "public" dialogue, I mean making their conclusions and their reasoning "accessible" to others in the organization. "Public" is the opposite of talking privately to a few friends about such issues. It means saying in a public forum, (staff meeting, team meeting, town hall, and so on) "Here is a concern I have, what do others think about it?" It may mean saying it more than once. It may also mean creating public forums that provide the opportunity for bringing multiple perspectives to bear on the ends that have been established for the organization, (for example, dialogue groups, intra-net discussion groups, book review groups, brown bag lunch meetings).

There has been an unwritten practice in organizations that if an organizational member does not agree with the direction the organization is taking, he or she can (or should) leave. While leaving is an option, leaving does little to help organizations deal with the difficult question of making sure the ends it serves are appropriate. It is only by staying and giving voice to concerns that such issues are ultimately addressed.

TIMING THE DIALOGUE

In this section, I deal with the issues of when to use dialogue in an organizational setting. A central issue is whether to set aside a specific time for dialogue or to attempt to be more dialogic in all our on-going interactions. Although I have posed it as an "either/or" issue, I think the compromise lies in "both/and". I believe it is necessary for a group to set aside some time for being in dialogue together, particularly initially. However, over time, the learning that comes from dialogue, affects all conversations. That is to say, members become more dialogic in all their interactions with each other, for example, they are more cognizant of their own assumptions, listen more carefully to others, challenge the status quo, inquire into one other's thinking rather than assuming they know what the other is thinking. If the effect of dialogue was to be felt only within meetings designated as "dialogue session", it will have not lived up to its potential.

Beginning with dialogue

A number of organizations have developed a variation of dialogue that occurs at the beginning and/or ending of each day. In some organizations, it functions as a kind of "check in". Each member speaks for a minute or two about what is current or "present" for him or her. The speeches are made to the centre of the circle, not in response to another member or *to* another member, and it is always acceptable to "pass". These "check in" times of 15-20 minutes allow people to note an issue that is troubling them, to share the joy of a "kid that won the game," to express a hoped for outcome of a project, to say what ever is noteworthy at the moment.

The "check in" is not really a dialogue from the perspective of any of the five theorists discussed in this book. Yet it has within it dialogic elements, in that it is a reminder that we relate to each other as whole person to whole person, and that we bring all of us to work each day. It can promote a dialogical attitude within the work setting that may allow our other conversations to become more dialogic.

A navy officer at the Pentagon told me about a variation on the "check in". This group of seven officers worked in the same office area, but over time came to realize that they knew little about the projects each was working on. One response to that realization was to take down many of the interior walls so that they could see and hear each other at work. (Research on space shows that we are all more likely to collaborate with those we can see.) However, of equal importance to the space changes was that this group began to dialogue. That came about due to the inordinate Washington DC traffic which caused them all to arrive an hour earlier than work was actually supposed to begin. By almost unspoken agreement, they set aside that hour to dialogue. Sometimes the dialogue touched on the personal but more often officemates talked about a project that was important to them or to speak about the frustration of an outcome that continued to elude them. At the end of the hour, everyone turned to their desk and began the day's work – but with a greater of sense of how their work fitted together and sometimes even how they might assist each other.

Interspersing dialogue

Having initially introduced dialogue to a group and perhaps held one or two dialogue practice sessions, it is possible for the group to elect to hold a dialogue periodically. That might occur when the group is stuck or polarized around a topic or when there is a difficult issue coming up on the agenda. Then a member of the group might suggest, "Let's hold a dialogue on this issue". It is helpful to set a period for how long the dialogue will last and, of course, to move into a circle for the time of the dialogue. Doris Adams at Trinity College uses this simple set of guidelines for such periodic times of dialogue:

1 Speak from your own experience (use "I" not "we", "you", or "people").
2 Practice "generative" listening (i.e. listening to learn from the other).
3 Suspend judgment when listening to the other.
4 Avoid "cross talk" - talk to the whole group rather than another member of the group.
5 Give up advice giving and problem solving.
6 Let silence create spaces for reflection between each person's speaking.

I like the simplicity of having only a few guidelines rather than having hard and fast rules or holding lengthy training sessions. I find participants can get overly concerned with "Are we doing it yet?" or "Are we doing it right?" and that concern can even sometimes prevent them from talking at a meaningful level.

Moreover, by keeping the guidelines simple, participants who begin to enact these guidelines during their times of dialogue, may find that they are more often using the guidelines in other meeting situations as well. So that over time their regular conversations become more dialogic and the differences between dialogue and other conversations becomes less pronounced.

THE QUESTION OF FACILITATION

I have thus far avoided talking about facilitation, perhaps in large part because I am so ambivalent about it. Yet, I acknowledge that in many of the activities described in this chapter I assume a facilitator, even without specifically refering to one. The question then is does dialogue require a facilitator and if so what kind of facilitation is helpful?

We have all been in groups that have been facilitated and thus recognize the broad range of possible tasks that a facilitator might take on:

- assist the group with issues of group dynamics (for example, dealing with a member who takes too much air time)
- serve as a safeguard to prevent group members from inflicting psychological pain on other members
- serve as a reflection or mirror for the group (for example, reflect back to the group observations about how they are functioning)
- serve as an expert on what is and is not acceptable in dialogue (for example, suggest that members talk to the centre of the room rather than addressing another member of the group)
- model the skills that others are expected to use
- create a "holding environment" for the group.

A group might find any of these helpful. However, I think the most important function is the last on the list, to create a "holding environment" for the group. I like the image that "holding" brings to mind. I picture two hands cupped, supporting and sheltering a group of people held within them. The image is one of strength yet great restraint or non-interference. A "holding environment" takes into account the structure, size, level of formality, shape, and to some extent, the rules of engagement, of the group. Most importantly, it involves setting the tone or spirit of the dialogue. I would hope a facilitator would manifest the underlying values of dialogue in the tone and respect with which he or she interacts with others on a daily basis – not just when the group meets at a designated time of dialogue. As the writing of Bohm, Argyris, Freire, Mezirow, Johnson and Johnson, and I hope my own illustrates, dialogue is as much a way of thinking about self in relation to others as it is about word choice or rules for interaction. The most critical facilitation task is to be aware of how those relationships within the group are being manifested, both implicitly and explicitly, through all the means individuals use to express their relationship with others. And by sharing that awareness, help the group remove those things that keep them from being in dialogue with each other.

My ambivalence about facilitation is that if a group has a designated facilitator, it is a great temptation to leave it to the facilitator to notice and correct the things that keep the group from being in dialogue, rather than the group taking that responsibility upon themselves. For example, during a dialogue a member might think to herself, "We've gone over and over this topic, why doesn't the facilitator have us move on?" rather than herself saying to the group, "I find myself tuning out because we have already talked these issues through. Are others still finding this topic of interest?" Because dialogue is about such things as examining one's own assumptions, making use of a wide diversity of ideas, and challenging prevailing ideas, leaving the "noticing" to one designated person is counter productive. There can be important learning for the group in understanding why a topic is continually revisited or in discovering what is being avoided by not "moving on." But such valuable learning comes from the noticing and engaging with those issues, not from the act of "moving on". That is why a facilitator cannot "do it for the group", as much as the group might wish it so.

We all recognize that "engaging" leaves us open to embarrassment and misinterpretation, so, when there is a designated facilitator, it is tempting to leave such engaging to the facilitator. "After all," we say to ourselves, "who am I to tell the group to move on, that's his job." The great danger of facilitation is that it significantly reduces the group's learning.

Ideally, a facilitator models the skills, (e.g. the noticing, the stage setting, and so on) for a period of time and then works him or herself out of a job as the members of the group gradually take over the facilitation role themselves. However, the reality is that both facilitator and group members tend to hang on to the status quo. For the facilitator it is very difficult to relinquish such an attractive role as the "wise and insightful" person. Especially when others come up to you afterward and say, "I'm really glad you said that in the group." Or "I don't know how you see those things that just go over the heads of the rest of us." Who wouldn't want to hang on to such a valued role? Likewise, group members themselves are reluctant to give up the protection from embarrassment and discomfort that the facilitator affords them. With both parties benefiting from the continuation, it is very difficult to stop.

If a group chooses to have a facilitator, I suggest that the group make a deliberate contract with that person

about the role he or she will play and about the length of
time for the facilitation. Which of the roles (from the list
above) does the group want the facilitator to fulfill? Which
is the group already skilful at and therefore could exercise
if it chose? It is also important that the contract with the
facilitator be revisited from time to time. Has the facilitator
moved beyond the roles specified in the contract? What
tasks is the group ready to take on that the facilitator has
been doing? What new help does the group need from the
facilitator? Is the group gaining facilitation ability itself or
tending to relinquish those tasks to the facilitator?

Facilitation for groups learning Argyris' Model II skills

There are two confusions about the work of Chris
Argyris that I want to address here because it is a special
case. One is that Argyris' Model II skills require an expert
in order to use and the second is that Argyris' dialogue
requires a written case. The confusion comes from the
difference in how one learns the skills and the on-going
use of the skills. I address each separately here,
particularly as it regards facilitation.

Learning/studying/practising to gain or improve the skills

For people to learn Model II skills they must be willing
closely to examine their own speech patterns to see how
they may be reducing their own learning in situations of
conflict. The way Argyris suggests doing that is to write out
the dialogue from a difficult situation and include in the
left-hand column what the case writer was thinking or
feeling but not saying. Then a small group of people who
are also attempting to learn the skills, get together to help
the case writer see what she cannot see for herself. While
discussing the case group members have the opportunity

to practice their own Model II skills and to examine their own assumptions. It is critical to the learning process to have an expert in Argyris' concepts present who can recognize the Model I traps we typically fall into and who can apply the speech patterns of Model II to the situation being discussed. Having a case analyzed in this way can be a bit disconcerting for the case writer who comes to realize that others can see the patterns the case writer characteristically uses, but of which she is unaware.

Using Model II skills in dialogue

Assuming that a member of a group has learned the Argyris' Model II skills (advocacy with inquiry, offering one's own reasoning, and publicly testing inferences) that member could use those skills in any interaction with others in order to learn better from others and to explain better his or her own ideas. For example, the member who feels strongly about a position might, because of her experience with the Argyris concepts, recognize that there may be things happening of which she is unaware. So rather than just advocating her position, she uses Model II skills to: (1) state her position, (2) give her reasoning, and (3) indicate that she is open to "disconfirmation". For example, "I think we should get the proposal in by January 14th so that we give ourselves at least a week to send it around for a quality check. Are there other considerations I am not taking into account?" By including the final question (Are there other considerations I am not taking into account?) in her statement, she goes beyond simply being willing to hear that she is wrong, to seeking actively any data that might disconfirm her opinion.

Group members make use of the Model II skills because it allows them to be more effective human beings, consultants, friends, and colleagues when in dialogue with others. However, in these situations, the member would not say, "I am using Model II now", nor would the member require that others know or learn Model II skills. Nor, would the everyday use of Model II skills involve writing out a case.

Nevertheless, of course, a member cannot use these skills if they have not practised them in a group as described above. The learning requires an expert facilitator and the use of left/right hand column cases. The on-going use of Model II in dialogue requires neither.

IMPROVING THE DIALOGUE

As a group talks together, over time, their conversations will inevitably change. Members learn to accommodate each other, to build patterns of interaction that are comfortable, to know what to expect of others and what others expect of them. Such changes bring ease, but they do not necessarily improve the dialogue. Dialogue improves as a result of the group intentionally focusing on how they are interacting and how they are deriving meaning from what is being said. Often that demands that the group be able to stand outside of the dialogue in order to look at it from a new or different perspective. One way to get that perspective is to have the help of a facilitator, with all the necessary cautions outlined above. In this section, I suggest other ways to gain that needed perspective.

Reflecting on dialogue

After a group has been in dialogue for thirty minutes or more, it is beneficial for them to take ten minutes to reflect on how they have been functioning. This allows the group to assess itself and to think about how to improve its dialogue. Certainly any comment participants make in this reflection time is acceptable. However, often what most quickly comes to mind for participants are evaluative comments, "I thought it went well" or "I enjoyed it". These are welcome comments, but often not very helpful for improvement. To get more depth in the reflection it may be useful to ask participants to consider a more specific question, although still open ended, for example:

- How do the periods of silence feel?
- What is making the dialogue meaningful for them?
- What makes it difficult for individuals to get into the conversation?
- How are participants experiencing suspending their own assumptions?
- Are there important patterns that occur over the dialogue time?
- What didn't you say that you wish you had said?

In these times of reflection, participants have a tendency to slide back into the content of the dialogue rather than reflecting *on the dialogue*, perhaps because the one so naturally leads to the other. A useful technique to facilitate the separation of the reflection from the content is to ask participants to stand behind their chairs for the reflection period. In this way, you are asking them to physically be in a different place in order to look back on what was said and how they reacted. It may be helpful, as well, to change the format of speaking. In dialogue there is typically no set sequence to who speaks next. For contrast, it may be helpful in reflecting on the dialogue to progress around the circle asking each person to offer a comment.

Even given these differences participants frequently find themselves enjoined in the dialogue again. Paradoxically, this conversation is often a more open and meaningful exchange than the original dialogue. It can be instructive to the group to contrast the reflection period with the dialogue itself to see what can be learned from the differences.

Video taping of dialogue

If we could "but see ourselves as others see us" - and, of course, through the miracle of videotape we can. By placing a camera far enough away from the group, the camera can be turned on and just left to run without anyone having to direct the shots. For the sake of getting everyone in the picture, the group may want to modify their usual circle to a "U" during video taping.

Video taping the dialogue is an extraordinarily helpful activity for a group to use periodically. It provides insights that a group can get in no other way. The value of video taping a dialogue is, of course, not in the taping, but in taking the time to reflect on the tape. I use a 3:1 ratio in planning time for the reflection, for example, for 30 minutes of taped dialogue I would allow about an hour and a half to watch and reflect on what was said. The reflection period seems to work best when a short segment of the tape is played and then the tape is stopped to consider what happened in that portion – then to play a bit more and stop again. Initially a facilitator may need to demonstrate stopping the tape, but participants soon feel free to call out "stop the tape" at a point they want to talk about.

For groups new to reflecting on their dialogue, it may be helpful to identify certain things to watch for in the tape. It is, of course, useful to look at the typical group process issues: Who talks? How much? Who interrupts whom? What comments do others respond to? What comments are dropped or ignored? Nevertheless, it is also possible to go deeper and ask participants: "At this point in the tape what assumptions were you making? "What was your internal response to that comment?" "If what Mary said was confusing what prevented others from asking her for clarification?"

Most groups prefer to erase the tapes immediately after they have used them for their own reflection. But if the group permits, it may also be useful to keep tapes for comparison purposes; that is, to consider how the group functioned six months ago versus now. A group may notice, for example, that there is more silence or that the group stays on a single topic longer in subsequent tapes.

Paired reflection

One of the most useful ways for a group to get some insight into its own dialogue practices is to make contact with another group that is also trying to improve their practices. The two groups get together. One group has a dialogue for 30 minutes or so while their partner group observes them in action. I like to place the partner group in a concentric circle around the dialogue group. At the end of the dialogue, the partner group offers their reflections on the dialogue. The two groups then switch roles and repeat the process, with the inner circle becoming the outer circle. One of the things I like about this way of gaining insight about a group's dialogue practices is that there is no built in teacher/pupil or expert/learner dichotomy. Rather the assumption is that both groups are learners and both are teachers. That is, each has useful insights to offer to the other. It is also an acknowledgement that others can see what we cannot see for ourselves.

In order to make the dialogue sessions as real as possible, I usually ask groups to take up an issue they have been addressing in a previous meeting. It is difficult to not to be "on your best behaviour" when someone else is watching. However, even given this obvious limitation, I find groups gain tremendous insight from this exchange. They learn from the reflections of the other group, from watching the other group in action, and from the exchange that occurs afterward when both groups talk about the difficulties and benefits of dialogue.

THE PARADOX OF DIALOGUE

I have, as you undoubtedly realize by now, great faith in dialogue. I believe it holds great promise for our fragile development as individuals and is necessary for the long deferred development of organizations. Yet, there remains a paradox for me. Ultimately, it is just "talk" that we must rely upon for something of such importance. I end, then, with a poem that contemplates that paradox.

> Amid complexity and strife
> With no clear path at hand,
> When trusted answers won't suffice
> How then to understand?

> Complexity to discourse turns.
> We've naught but this poor tool
> Of fervent words in counterpoint
> Uncertainty to school.

Then heed the voices of dissent,
Yet honour sanctioned thought
And strain to hear what's left unsaid
And challenge what is not.

There's knowing at the heart of this
Cacophony of sound.
Through insight borne of dissonance
Rare clarity is found.

The paradox of dialogue;
That simple talk can yield
An understanding so profound
Shared wisdom is revealed.

Sources for chapter 7

[1] Bird F B and Waters J A 'The Moral Muteness of Managers *California Management Review* Fall 1989: 32,1, pp.73-88.

[2] Wild H, Bishop L and Sullivan C L (1996) *Building Environments for Learning and Innovation* Institute for Research on Learning.

Index

Ackoff, R.
  democratic corporation,
    proposal for, 13
Action Learning
  development of, 88-90
  purpose and process, 88-89
  underlying principles, 89-90
Activity
  raising undiscussables,
    107-110
  right/left hand column cases,
    110-112
Adams, Doris
  periodic times of dialogue,
    117
Adult development
  differentiated perspective,
    8-9
  integrated perspective, 8-9
  open perspective, 8-9
  support for re-framing, 9
Agent of development
  dialogue as, 78-80
Alinsky, Saul
  emancipatory tradition of, 34
Argyris, Chris
  defensive routines, on, 10
  Model I, 22
  Model II skills.
    See Model II skills
  organizational learning,
    work on, 21-28

purpose of dialogue, 60
Beer, Stafford
  team syntegrity, process of,
    91-92
Beginning with dialogue,
  115-116
Berger, Peter, 12
Bird, F.B.
  moral muteness of
    managers, on, 99
Bohm, David
  dissolving programmes,
    concept of, 31, 37
  instrumental relationships,
    avoidance of, 65, 64
  purpose of dialogue, 60
  shared meaning,
    development of, 28-33
Brookfield, Stephen
  understanding motives, on,
    61-62
Buber, Martin, 64

Chilean Institute for Agrarian
  Reform, 50
Circle
  arrangement of seating in,
    101-102
Co-operation and productivity
  benefits, 39-40
  positive outcomes,
    conditions for,

cognitive processes,
44-45
controversy, 45-48
generally, 41-42, 48
information exchange, 44-45
positive interdependence, 42
promotive interaction,
43-44
social skills, 42
process, 49
process gain, 40-41
purpose, 49
reasoning strategies, 40
skills and attitudes, 49
social interdependence,
theory of, 39
studies on productivity, 40
summary, 49
target audience, 49
transfer of learning, 41
Cognitive processes
promotive interaction,
elements of, 44-45
Cohen, Morris, 14-15
Communicative learning
nature of, 35-37
Complexity
development as necessary
response to, 11-13
Conditions
dialogue of, 92-94
productive dialogue, for,
31-33
rational discourse, for, 34-39
viable dialogue, for,
collective intelligence, 76-77
empowerment of group, 75
equality among participants,
75-76
generally, 74-75
mixed interactions, 77
Conference
future search, 85-86

open space, 86-87
Consensual validation
process of, 36-37
Controversy
promotive interaction,
elements of, 45-48
Creating dialogue
dialoguing about what
matters, 113-114
knowing how to talk,
106-107
limits on talk, 105-106
means and ends
conversations, 113-114
raising undiscussables,
107-110
right/left hand column cases,
110-112
Critical thinking
naive thinking distinguished
from, 54

Defensive routines
nature of, 10
Deutsch, Morton
social interdependence,
theory of, 39
Development
agent of, dialogue as, 78-80
complexity, dealing with,
11-13
individual.
See Individual development
meaning, 11
organizational.
See Organizational
development
Developmental talk.
See Dialogue
Dialogue
co-operation. See Co-
operation and productivity
conditions of, 92-94

creating.
>*See* Creating dialogue
discussion compared with,30
facilitation, question of,
>118-123
improving.
>*See* Improving dialogue
intellectual capability,
>affirmation of, 66-67
meaning, 59-60, 30, 2
misleading others, 13-14
organizational learning.
>*See* Organizational
>>learning
paradox of, 127-128, 68
people's knowledge of, 62
productive, conditions for,
>31-33
productivity. *See* Co-
>operation and productivity
purpose of, 60-61
rational discourse.
>*See* Rational discourse
relationship, as, 63-64
saying more than one knows,
>14-15
saying nothing, 15-16
shared meaning.
>*See* Shared meaning
situation variables in, 94
skilled talk distinguished
>from, 1
speech acts in, 93
structuring.
>*See* Structuring dialogue
timing. *See* Timing dialogue
transformation.
>*See* Transformation
unpredictable outcome of, 67
Differentiated
>meaning, 8
Discussion
>dialogue compared with, 30

meaning, 30
rational discourse.
>*See* Rational discourse

Emancipatory learning
>nature of, 37
Employee
>use of term, 64

Facilitation
>groups learning Argyris'
Model II skills, 121-123
>holding environment,
>>118-119
>question of, 118-121
>tasks of facilitator, 118
Faith
>need for, 53
Forums for dialogue
>action learning,
>>development of, 88
>>purpose and process, 88-89
>>underlying principles,
>>>89-90
>agent of development,
>>dialogue as, 78-80
>container, as, 77-78
>emergence of, 73-81
>future search conferences,
>>85-86
>generally, 85
>open space technology,
>>86-87
>real-time strategic change,
>>90-91
>team syntegrity,
>>91-92
>viable dialogue,
>>conditions for,
>>collective intelligence,
>>>76-77
>>empowerment of group, 75
>>equality among

participants, 75-76
generally, 74-75
mixed interactions, 77
Freire, Paulo
emancipatory tradition of, 34
need for humility, on, 15
purpose of dialogue, 60
requirements for dialogue, 63
52-54
transformation, work on,
50-54
Fromm, Erich, 50
Fuller, Buckminster
Team Syntegrity, basis of, 91
Future search conference
elements of, 85-86
purpose of, 85
work of, 86

Great Books discussion
groups, 3
Groups
learning, role of others in,
61-62
size for speaking and
reflecting, 102-103
See also Forums for dialogue
Guevara, Che, 50

Habermas, Jurgen, 34
Handy, C.
shamrock organization,
proposal for, 13
Haworth, 104-105
Hitachi America Ltd, 104
Hope
need for, 53
Human resource
use of term, 64
Humility
need for, 15, 52-53

Improving dialogue

generally, 123
paired reflection, 126-127
reflecting on dialogue,
123-125
video taping of dialogue,
125-126
Individual development
being oneself at work, 13-14
differentiated perspective,
8-9
integrated perspective, 8-9
open perspective, 8-9
support for re-framing, 9
team, concept of, 8
Information exchange
promotive interaction,
elements of, 44-45
Instrumental learning
nature of, 35
Integrated
meaning, 8
Intellectual capability
dialogue as affirmation of,
66-67
Interaction practices.
See Model II skills
Interspersing dialogue, 117

Johnson, David, 39-48, 60
Johnson, Roger, 39-48, 60
Jung, Carl
truth, on, 14

Kegan, Robert, 1, 12
King, Martin Luther, 50
Kuhn, Thomas, 12

Learning
communicative, 35-37
development, and, 10
emancipatory, 37
instrumental, 35
organizational,

interaction practices, 23-27
limitations on, 21-23
summary, 28
role of others in, 61-62
talk, dependent on,10
transfer of, 41
types of, 34-38
Lorde, Audre
silence, on, 15
Love
need for, 53

Managers
moral muteness of, 99
Mao Tse-tung, 50
Mezirow, Jack
purpose of dialogue, 60
rational discourse,
conditions for, 34-39
Model II skills
choice, 27
embarrassment, risk of, 24
facilitation for groups
learning, 121-123
generally, 23-24
governing variables, 26
implementation, 24-26
losing, risk of, 24
process, 28
purpose, 28
right/left hand column cases,
110-112
skills and attitudes, 28
summary, 28
target audience, 28
types of, 23
valid information, 26-27

Naive thinking
critical thinking
distinguished from, 54
National City Bank, 104

Open
meaning, 8
Open space technology
purpose, 86-87
rules for, 87
Organizational development
agent of, dialogue as,
78-80
complexity, response to,
11-13
defensive routines, 10
learning and development, 10
new forms of structure,
search for, 13
Organizational learning
interaction practices, 23-27
limitations on, 21-23
summary, 28
Organizational talk
game-like quality of, 7
limitations of, 7-8
Organizations
dialogue practices in, 99-128
Ortega y Gasset, Jose, 50
Owen, Harrison
open space technology,
86-87
Owens Corning, 104

Paired reflection, 126-127
Paradox of dialogue, 68,
127-128
Positive interdependence
existence of, 42
Process gain
co-operative action,
benefits of, 40-41
Productive dialogue
conditions for, 31-33
Productivity.
See Co-operation
and productivity
Programmes

construction of, 28-29, 31
Promotive interaction
elements of, 43-44
meaning, 43
Public dialogue
meaning, 114

Quality control
instrumental learning,
application of, 35

Raising undiscussables,
107-110
Rational discourse
communicative learning,
35-37
conditions for, 34-39
consensual validation, 36-37
emancipatory learning, 37
instrumental learning, 35
learning,
communicative, 35-37
emancipatory, 37
instrumental, 35
types of, 34-38
process, 38
purpose, 38
skills and attitudes, 38
summary, 38-39
target audience, 39
Re-framing
support for, 9
Real-time strategic change
process of, 90-91
Reasoning strategies
co-operative action,
benefits of, 40
Reflecting on dialogue,
123-125
Relationship
dialogue as, 63-64
Revans, Reginald
Action Learning,

development of, 88-90

SAS Airlines, 104
Sartre, Jean-Paul, 50
Shared meaning
development of, 28-34
fragmentary view of world,
29-30
process, 33-34
productive dialogue,
conditions for, 31-33
programmes,
construction of, 28-29, 31
purpose, 33
skills and attitudes, 33
society must be based on, 30
summary, 33-34
Siemens, 105
Silence
development, effect on,
15-16
Situation variables in dialogue,
94
Size of group, 102-103
Social skills
productivity, effect on, 42
Society
shared meaning, based on, 30
Speech acts in dialogue, 93
Steelcase Corporation, 103-104
Structuring dialogue
circle, arrangement of
seating in, 101-102
making space for dialogue,
103-105
size of group, 102-103
surroundings, impact of, 100
Support for re-framing, 9

Talk
developmental. See Dialogue
learning dependent on, 10
organizational, 7-8

skilled, distinguished from
developmental talk, 1
Team
  concept of, 8
Team syntegrity
  process of, 91-92
Timing dialogue
  beginning with dialogue,
    115-116
  importance of, 115
  interspersing dialogue, 117
Transfer of learning
  co-operative action,
    benefits of, 41
Transformation
  critical thinking, need for, 54
  faith, need for, 53
  hope, need for, 53
  humility, need for, 52-53
  love, need for, 53
  process of, 50-52
  process, 54
  purpose, 54
  rational perspective, 52-54
  skills and attitudes, 54
  summary, 54
  target audience, 54

UNESCO, 50
United States of America
  dialogue groups,
    formation of, 2

Unpredictability of dialogue,
  67

Video taping of dialogue,
  125-126

Waters, J.A.
  moral muteness of
    managers, on, 99
Weisbord, Marvin
  future search conferences,
    85-86
Work processes
  agent of development,
    dialogue as, 78-80
  container, forum as, 77-78
  incorporation of
    dialogue into, 73-81
  viable dialogue,
    conditions for,
  collective intelligence, 76-77
  empowerment of group, 75
  equality among participants,
    75-76
  generally, 74-75
  mixed interactions, 77
Work relationships
  human resource,
    use of term, 64
  instrumental nature of,
    effect of dialogue on, 64-65

An invitation to keep in touch

To receive the latest information on forthcoming titles and developments in the Library please return this coupon to our London office at the address below. Also if you would like to comment on our books in any way, we would be happy to hear from you.

--- ✂

☐ Please include me on the Mike Pedler Library mailing list.

Mr/Ms/Mrs/Miss   First name _____

Surname _____

Position / Organization _____

Department _____

Address _____

_____

_____

Country _____

Postcode _____ Tel _____

Lemos&Crane
20 Pond Square
Highgate Village
London N6 6BA England
Tel: +44 (0)181 348 8263
Fax: +44(0)181 347 5740
E-mail: admin@lemos.demon.co.uk

Also published in the Mike Pedler Library

ABC of Action Learning

Professor Reg Revans in this new edition of his classic *ABC of Action Learning* distils the lessons of decades of experience applying the theory he originated - Action Learning - the most important idea to have emerged in management and organizational development since the war. Revans' lifelong mission has been to empower all managers in all organizations to act and to learn from action. The *ABC of Action Learning* sets out practical means of realising his vision. In today's rapidly changing environment where learning is needed to innovate constantly, Revans' ideas are more relevant than ever.

ABC of Action Learning gives you:
- structures to implement action learning programmes based on an understanding of its operational forms
- insights gained from experiences of launching action learning world-wide and responses of top management to efforts to improve their own enterprises
- conditions for bringing about learning in the organization as a whole system.

Professor Reg Revans, creator of action learning, is one of the UK's original business thinkers. A member of the pioneering management team at the National Coal Board after the war, appointed as Britain's first professor of industrial administration in the 1960s, Reg Revans has worked with managers in Britain, Europe, America, Africa and India. He was recently made a Freeman of the City of London.

"interest in Revans' ideas pours in from around the world"
Financial Times

ISBN 1-898001-42-1

Also published in the Mike Pedler Library

Resolving Conflicts in Organizations

Conflicts are common in organizations. Why do conflicts escalate? And how can they be resolved? **Dame Rennie Fritchie** and **Malcolm Leary** set out tried-and-tested approaches to help you understand the nature of conflicts in organizations and to implement strategies to resolve them. Working through the text with an example of conflict from your own experience, *Resolving Conflicts in Organizations* will give you:

- a framework to recognise the characteristics of a particular conflict - 'hot' or 'cold' - and how individual temperaments react to different kinds of conflict

- an understanding of how conflicts in groups can escalate - from discussion through to destruction

- the skills needed to resolve conflict at different levels of escalation through changing behaviour, attitude and perception.

Dame Rennie Fritchie's career has spanned insurance, industrial training boards, finance, consulting and health. For almost a decade she held chairing roles in the National Health Service and was a member of the National Policy Group. She is the author of *The Business of Assertiveness*. Her co-author **Malcolm Leary** is a consultant and researcher with many clients in the UK and throughout the world. He is the co-founder of Transform and a partner, along with Dame Rennie Fritchie, of The Conflict Challenge.

ISBN 1-898001-45-6

Also published in the Mike Pedler Library

A Concise Guide to the Learning Organization

Creating and developing learning organizations is an essential quest. But much of the available guidance is criticised for being long-winded and difficult to implement. Now, in *A Concise Guide to the Learning Organization*, **Dr Mike Pedler** and **Kath Aspinwall** show leaders and managers facing unprecedented and unpredictable change how to understand, embrace and harness practical principles, models and approaches that will enhance any organization's capacity to learn. Case examples and "snapshots" of organizations working towards learning are used throughout the book - as are activities that help you evaluate levels of development within your organization.

A Concise Guide to the Learning Organization gives you:

- a practical understanding of the nature of learning and organizational learning, and how the principles of the Eleven Characteristics of the Learning Company can be applied

- an appreciation of the blocks to learning, its limitations, and the shadow side of organizations

- ideas for future development - how learning organizations can contribute to the wider environment, their vital role in the creation of the Good Society.

Dr Mike Pedler, series editor of The Mike Pedler Library, is an adviser to some of Britain's leading companies, Revans Professorial Fellow at the University of Salford, visiting professor at the University of York, co-author of the best-selling *Managing Yourself, A Manager's Guide to Self-development* and *The Learning Company*. His co-author, **Kath Aspinwall**, is a lecturer in education management at Sheffield Hallam University and author (with Mike Pedler) of *Perfect plc?* and *Leading the Learning School*.

ISBN 1-898001-43-X